A Guide to Japanese Pubs and Izakaya

東京居酒屋ガイド

島本 慶 Kei Shimamoto & SKIP

Bilingual Edition
What to Do at Night in Tokyo

The personalities of the owner, chef, manager even the kitchen helper, waiter, and waitress become the most crucial element to an Izakaya.

Counters are usually occupied by the customers that come alone. Many of these customers become regulars. They visit the same place and sit at the same spot every day. Some even earn the honor of having the same seat reserved for them.

No matter how close the customers and the staff seem to be, there remains a fine line of respect and delicacy. The restaurants always stay polite and sensitive to the customer's needs and privacy.

Instead of dining in a big box, these downtown Izakayas remain down to earth and have kept the human touch and the quiet atmosphere of traditional Japan.

Izakya has been acting as a communication place for Japanese since the ancient times. Especially those who work in a company or belong to some activity groups probably have spent some time in Izakaya with their coworkers or friends while extending their chopsticks over delicious food and drinks. This promotes and tightens the bond of a group.

There's no set style for an Izakaya restaurant. Different from high-end restaurants and Japanese kaiseki restaurant, Izakaya is priced reasonably and has a casual atmosphere. Most places are open until late at night so you can sit back and relax without worrying about the time.

Through Izakaya, you will discover the true nature of Japanese and their love for peace and harmony and the charm of this unique pub culture.

Contents

Foreword まえがき 10

The History of Izakaya 居酒屋の歴史 12

What is Izakaya for Japanese People? 日本人と居酒屋とは 16

Manners in Izakaya 居酒屋でのマナー 18

Izakaya Special Selection 55 in Tokyo 東京の居酒屋特選 55 軒

East Area 東部地区 24

West Area 西部地区 54

South Area 南部地区 90

North Area 北部地区 118

Appendix

1, Shinjuku Golden Gai　新宿ゴールデン街 142

2, Iakaya Menu　居酒屋メニュー 150

Foreword まえがき

People say food and the drink are the most important things for Izakaya. However, that's not true. Like any business, Izakaya is a business involving people. Therefore, the personalities of the owner, chef, manager even the kitchen helper, waiter, and waitress become the most crucial element to an Izakaya. The personalities of these people contribute to the success and how comfortable an Izakaya is.

For a long time there has been the word "kanbanmusume". "musume" means "daughter" or "young lady." So kanban musume means "poster girl" of shops/restaurants. Their friendly and usually cute appearances give good impressions to the customers. Nowadays, the male staffs have also become an important component in terms of providing hospitality and comfort to the customers.

Counter and table seating and tatami room are always found in Izakaya. Counters are usually occupied by the customers that come alone. With the rise of unmarried people, both single men and women go to Izakaya without a company and have a drink alone.

Many of these customers become regulars. They visit the same place and sit at the same spot every day. Some even earn the honor of having the same seat reserved for them.

No matter how close the customers and the staff seem to be, there remains a fine line of respect and delicacy. The restaurants always stay polite and sensitive to the customer's needs and privacy. As a result, elder men who are grieving for the loss of their wives would utilize Izakaya as their own kitchen.

People going to the public bath alone would stop by Izakaya on the way home. Watching TV and having a drink. A routine to finish the day for many people. It is almost like a ritual. A tradition that is said to have established during the Edo era.

Many Izakaya have remained in the downtown area. Very different from the big commercialized chain Izakaya found in front of the stations. Instead of dining in a big box, these downtown Izakayas remain down to earth and have kept the human touch and the quiet atmosphere of traditional Japan.

More and more foreigners are seen in Japan. It is my wish to share these perspectives with those visiting from overseas. An original Japanese Izakaya. To directly meet and be in contact with the local people and to experience and enjoy their warmth and hospitality. Through Izakaya, you will discover the true nature of Japanese and their love for peace and harmony and the charm of this unique pub culture.

　居酒屋で一番大切なことは酒と肴の旨さだと言いたいところだが、それは違って、その店で接客する女将たちや従業員たちのパーソナリティーなのだ。その個性がすなわち店の個性であり、その店の居心地具合を左右するからである。

　昔から言う、"看板娘"（女将の娘で、若くて可愛いキャラ）やおもてなしの気配りで気持ちよく接客する男性店員も大事な要素といえる。

　居酒屋の店内には必ずカウンターやテーブル席そして座敷というのがある。中でもそのカウンター席には独り客が陣取ることが多い。最近は未婚率も上がり独身男性、それも中高年の独り飲みや"お一人様"という独身女性も独りグラスを傾けるなんて姿も見かけるようになっている。

　そんな客の中にはほとんど毎日やってくる常連客がいて、場合によっては座るカウンター席の位置が決まっている名誉常連もいたりするものだ。

　当然従業員とは顔なじみだし、ほぼ店は家庭のような感覚と見ていい。かといって客と店という一線を越え、デリカシーを欠くほど気安く接客されることはなく、ほど良く心地よく接客されるものだからつい、女房に先立たれた独り暮らしの高齢者で自宅の台所のように使っている人たちを見かける。

　風呂も独りだから銭湯を利用して、ひとつ風呂浴びて店にやってくる。いつもの席で、テレビを見ながら晩酌をする。まるでそれは一日を終えるための儀式のように。このような風景は、本来あるべき江戸時代に確立した居酒屋の有るべき姿と言ってもいいだろう。

　そんな居酒屋が下町には数多く残っていて、駅前に必ずある大手チェーン店系の大箱では味わえない、静かな日本的な独特な雰囲気を漂わせている。

　海外からのお客さんも、最近ではよく見かけるが、このような本来あるべき姿の居酒屋を覗いていただきたい。そこには人と人とが触れあう、いわゆる庶民的な温もりを味わえるに違いない。日本人の心の一端を、垣間見るこができるかも知れない。

Kei Shimamoto　島本 慶

The History of Izakaya

Izakaya goes a long way back in Japanese history. The history of alcohol brewing dates back to the 8th century. With the development of a stable money system in the Nara period, temples started to brew sake and offer it for private consumption. Shrines followed thereafter.

Over time, from Heian period through Muromachi period, brewery house gradually became popular. Not only temples and shrines, merchants called "Jozoya" started to brew sake for commercial purpose. However, at the time, other than festivals, drinking was only limited to the wealthy aristocrats and not the common people as they had restrictions on consuming alcohols.

As the urban economic development took full swing during Kamakura era, "Jozoya" became wide spread throughout the country. Some brewery houses began selling sake to Bushi, the warrior class. Eventually, these Jozoya evolved into a business called Koshokuya which offered drinking and women prostitutes as well.

By the end of the Kamakura era, brewery houses gained economic strength from selling sake. It also became an important taxable commodity which brought significant incomes to the Bakufu government.

By this time, sake was sold to the common class people. And the business that used to only sell alcohols also became a financial institute on the side.

By the Muromachi era, "Sakaya" that specialized in selling sake were established.

Subsequently in the Sengoku period, feudal lords began to aggressively protect the "sakaya" as they predicted the

居酒屋の歴史

　日本人における居酒屋の歴史は古い。そもそも日本における酒の醸造が始まり定着したのが8世紀初頭とされている。そして奈良時代には貨幣経済の発達にともない寺院などで酒の醸造と提供が始まり、続いて神社でも行うようになっていったという。

　やがて平安時代から室町時代にかけて寺社だけでなく民間でも「醸造屋」と呼ばれる業者が酒の醸造を行うようになっていく。ただし提供する相手は、当時祭り以外での飲酒が法律で規制されていた庶民ではなく貴族階級の富裕層に限られていた。

　やがてこの「醸造屋」が全国に広がっていき、都市経済が本格化していった鎌倉時代には貴族以外の武士階級に酒を提供する「醸造屋」も登場するようになるのである。ただしこちらは飲酒だけでなく売春業も行われ別名「好色家」(こうしょくや)とも呼ばれていた。

　その後、鎌倉時代の末期になってようやく商人階級への酒類の提供が盛んになるにつれて「醸造屋」の経済力が増すと、幕府からは重要な課税対象とみなされるようになっていったのである。

　この頃になると、酒類の提供だけにとどまらず、同時に庶民相手の金融業も兼業するようになっていったという。

　やがて室町時代になると酒の量り売りだけを専門に行う「酒屋」が登場するようになっていった。

　続いて戦国時代になると各大名は領地内の経済強化を目論み、それら「酒屋」を積極的に保護す

significant effect these liquor shops played on economic development. Many shops were open in urban areas and along the roads catering to travelers.

Liquor shops were developed rapidly at the start of Edo era. Shops began not only selling alcohols, but began serving it on the spot. In addition, side dishes were added to the menus as well.

Moreover, places such as "niuriya" that sell dishes of simmered foods also began to serve sake. Small vendors started to sell sake and food in the portable stands which became the origin of today's Izakaya. The word Izakaya is a compound word consisting of "I" to stay and "sakaya" sake shop. It literally means a place to stay and drink.

In those days, 80% of the population in Edo was men. Because they were mostly single men, Izakaya that offered drinks and food became extremely wide spread. Eventually Izakaya became a place where people stopped for a drink and food.

During the Meiji era, foreign liquors such as beer and wine were introduced. Western style drinking place called "Ebisu Beer Hall" was established in Ginza catering to the wealthy people. Western-style Izakaya such as cafes and cabarets were opened one after another. From the end of WWII until 1970s, Izakaya became a sanctuary where office workers, especially men, smoked, drank and socialized. Later, as women gained status in society, Izakaya began to modify their menus and expanded their services to accommodate women and family customers.

Today, Izakaya has transformed into an eatery with rich menus and great services. It also represents a unique Japanese style pub where people can drink and eat food they like. It is a new style of eatery that is rarely seen around the world.

るようになり、次々と都市部や街道沿いには庶民相手の店が出店するようになっていくのである。

　この「酒屋」の本格的な発展は江戸時代に入って加速する。酒の量り売りだけでなくその場（店内）で酒を飲ませるようになっていくのである。さらに簡単な肴も提供するようになっていった。

　またその他にも小魚などの煮物を販売する「煮売屋」が酒を置くようになったり、屋台から発展したものなど様々な形態の「居酒屋」が江戸の街に登場し現在の居酒屋の原型がここに出来ていくのである。ちなみに「居酒屋」という名前の元々の意味は「酒屋で居続けて飲む」行為を意味する「居酒」（いざけ）の店の意味である。

　当時江戸の町の男女比率が極端に男性に偏っており（男８：女２）圧倒的に独身男性が多かったため、そのために酒が飲めて簡単に食事も摂れる居酒屋が爆発的に広まり、定着し、現在に至っているのである。

　そして明治時代になるとビールなどの洋酒が日本に流入し銀座に富裕層向けの「恵比寿ビアホール」が設立されたり、各地でカフェやキャバレーなどの洋風居酒屋が相次いで開店していくが、戦後から1970年代頃までは「居酒屋」といえばタバコの煙が充満する男性サラリーマン達が酒を飲む男の聖域と化していたのだが、それも近年の女性の社会進出に伴い、女性客や家族連れへの配慮から各店でメニューや飲み物の種類が豊富になったり、サービスに工夫を凝らしたお店が多くなり、現在のようななんでも好きなものを飲食できる世界的にみても極めて希な日本的な飲食店として進化していったのである。

What is Izakaya for Japanese people?

Izakya has been acting as a communication place for Japanese since the ancient times. Especially those who work in a company or belong to some activity groups probably have spent some time in Izakaya with their coworkers or friends while extending their chopsticks over delicious food and drinks. This promotes and tightens the bond of a group. It was a widely recognized practice during the high economic growth era in the 60's to 70's and even words such as "nomi-communication" were formed. Drinking and communicating became a norm and a vital social skill which were carried out in the public and the private sectors.

Japanese think it's impolite to speak directly. They consider it as a disgraceful act that lacks certain delicacy to say what's on their mind without precaution or prior notice. Therefore, they cherish the prelude of relaxing their body and mind before speaking the truth. Japanese reaffirm the community spirit and start any kind of social event with a shout of "Kanpai".

The local retirees exchange information with a happy smile on their face. Izakaya has been the place used widely by Japanese business men and women as a meeting spot, by couples as a date spot, and by housewives to temporarily step away from their busy daily chores. It is also a place to host commencement parties for the second or third generation successors in the neighborhood.

Moreover, the big izakaya located in the buildings of the terminal stations are good for hosting big parties. They have the capacity for large crowd to get together and celebrate various special occasions such as an after party of a wedding, a

日本人にとって居酒屋とは

　昔から居酒屋は日本人にとってコミュニケーションの場の一つとして機能している。特に会社や学校など何らかのグループに所属する大概の日本人にとって、グループ内の仲間と酒を酌み交わし、同じ皿の美味しい肴に舌鼓を打ってお互いの共同体意識を強固にするという方法は高度経済成長時代である60年代〜70年代には「飲みニュケーション」＝(飲む＋コミニュケーション)などという造語が生まれるほど一般的でオーソドックスな社交術として広く認識されていた。

　本音をしゃべることは、ある種デリカシーに欠けるはしたない行為と考え、建て前を大切にする日本人にとって、酔ってリラックスした言葉は腹を割って語られた本音として捕らえられるところもあり、日本人にとってこの居酒屋は「カンパーイ」のかけ声とともに始める共同体意識を確認する場所となっているのだ。

　顔をつきあわせ笑いながら地元のご隠居さん同士が情報交換をしたり、商店街の二代目三代目のお披露目や企業で働くサラリーマンやＯＬ、または家庭の主婦たちの息抜きの場や恋人たちのデートスポットとして大いに利用されている。

　またターミナル駅前のテナントビルなどに入っている大きな店なら、結婚式の2次会やサッカー応援団の飲み会、さらには同窓会に

reunion of friends and alumni, or simply a place to stop by after soccer games or before any festivals.

Finally, there's no set style for an Izakaya restaurant. Different from high-end restaurants and Japanese kaiseki restaurant, Izakaya is priced reasonably and has a casual atmosphere. Most places are open until late at night so you can sit back and relax without worrying about the time. And like any other restaurant in Japan, there is no discrimination towards a certain identity, occupation, gender, status or age. Whether you're blue-collar or white-collar, the same service and hospitality will be provided to you. Everybody is just as important as everyone else. You could say Izakaya might be the ideal place for not only the Japanese drinkers but anyone who wants to enjoy their drinks and be treated like a VIP.

Manners in Izakaya

As soon as being seated, even before placing any order, the waiter/waitress may bring a little appetizer in a small bowl called otoshi or tsukidashi. Otoshis is just a little something to munch on while you're deciding or waiting for your order. It is a relatively common practice in izakaya and is considered as the basic cover charge which will be included in your bill. They are usually for just a few hundred yen so it is polite not to reject it.

There are several taboos in handling chopsticks and here are a few to watch out for.

Don't lick your chopsticks even if there are food crumbs sticking on them. Don't dig or stab food with your chopsticks. Don't pass food from chopsticks to chopsticks. This is because it's a reminder of a custom used in Japanese funerals when

お祭りの打ちあげと、まぁ日本人にとってある種の晴れのパーティー会場としての役割も担っているのだ。

また居酒屋は高級なレストランや和食懐石料亭とは明らかに違いリーズナブルであり、夜遅くまで営業していて、時間を気にせず肩も凝らずに気軽に利用することができることも特徴として大きい。しかも日本における他の飲食店同様に一切の身分・職業・性別・年齢による区別も差別も無い。ブルーカラーもホワイトカラーも関係なく、ただただ大切なゲストとしておもてなしを受けるのだ。もはや日本の酒飲みだけでなく世界の酒飲みにとって、この居酒屋は天国と言ってもいいのかもしれない。

居酒屋でのマナー

席に座った途端に注文もしていないのに小鉢に入った料理を出されることが土地や店によってあるが、これは「お通し」や「突き出し」といって最初の注文した料理がくるまでの間をつなぐためのものだとされているが、いわばチャージのようなもの。それほど高額ではないので断らずに店に従うようにしたい。

箸の扱いで様々なタブーがあるが、代表的なものとして、舌先を舐める「舐り箸」。並ぶ料理の上でどれにしようかと箸先を泳がせる「迷い箸」や箸で摘んだ料理を相手

cremated bones are ceremoniously transferred from person to person into the urn.

Moreover, do not leave your chopsticks standing upright in your rice. This is like an incense offering for the death in Japanese Buddhist ceremony.

Also, when sharing a dish, put your share on your own plate instead of taking it directly from the large plate.

Do not make excessive orders or special requests in the preparation of your food, nor wolf it down. This can cause mistakes and add more time.

Finish all the food and drink you order. Don't pack the left over as it can cause food poisoning, especially in the case of raw fish, sashimi.

Always balance your order. Don't just order drinks. Izakaya is not just a bar, it is also a restaurant.

Finally, depending on the type and the size of the Izakaya, not all Izakaya are good for loud talking and rowdy parties. Please be selective and be considerate of others.

By the way, it is a good gesture to return the disposable chopsticks in the original paper envelop after finishing the meal, it will be appreciated by the staff when cleaning up as they won't get their hands dirty. However, make sure you don't put them back all the way but half way and fold the end of paper a little bit as a sign that the chopsticks had been used.

　の箸に渡す行為もタブー。これは火葬場で遺骨を骨壺に入れるときの箸の扱いと同じだからだ。

　またご飯に箸をまっすぐに突き立てる行為もよくない。これは日本の仏教において死者に対してご飯を供える方法である。

　また大皿から直接口に運ぶのも良くない。一旦自分の小皿に移してからいただきたい。

　それでは居酒屋の店員さんに対する行為で気を付けたいことはといえば、まずは注文を次々ということ。間違いの元であり、結局時間が掛かってしまう。

　そして飲み物や食べ物は残さないようにしたい。ついでに言うなら残った食べ物を無断で持ち帰らない。いくら新鮮な刺身でも何時間もたつと食中毒の原因にもなるかもしれない。

　かといってドリンクだけで料理を注文しないのも良くない。ここはバーではなく、居酒屋。美味しい料理とお酒をバランスよく注文したい。

　また店の規模に応じて騒げる店とそうじゃない店があるので、見極めたいところである。

　ちなみに、使い終わった箸は袋に戻して袋の先端を少し折り曲げておくのが正式なマナーで使用済みのサインになるし、店員さんの手が汚れないので、気の利く人だと思われること間違いなしだ。

翻訳：M.T. Edward Freeman
装幀：アキヨシアキラ　デザイン
DTP：ギルド
撮影：岩屋光俊、ヤマシタチカコ、佐藤真也
協力：双葉社刊　「週刊大衆」連載企画『おとなの居酒屋』

※掲載の内容は平成 27 年 6 月現在のものです。

Izakaya Special Selection

東京の居酒屋
特選55軒

55
in Tokyo

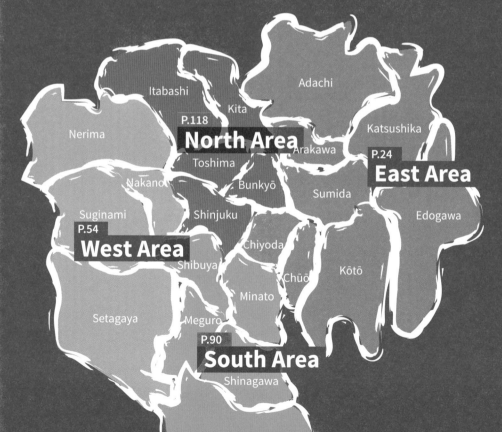

- P.118 **North Area**
- P.24 **East Area**
- P.54 **West Area**
- P.90 **South Area**

East Area

東部地区

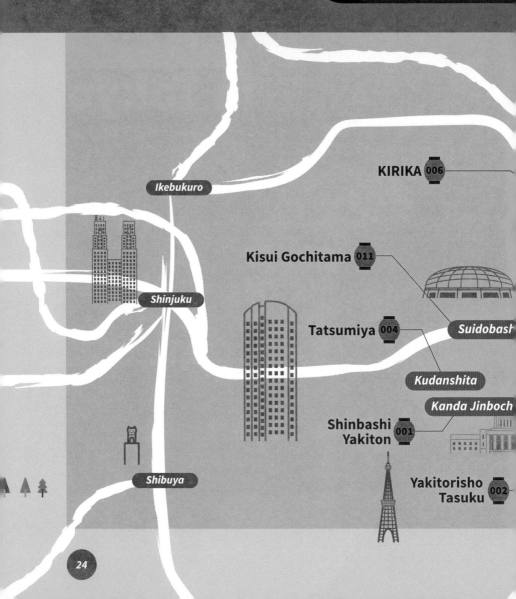

Adachi-ku（足立区）　Edogawa-ku（江戸川区）
Katsushika-ku（葛飾区）　Chiyoda-ku（千代田区）
Arakawa-ku（荒川区）　Chuo-ku（中央区）
Sumida-ku（墨田区）　Kōtō-ku（江東区）

01 Shinbashi Yakiton Kanda Jinbocho Branch

Kanda Jinbocho **Yakiton**

Hello Residence Jinbocho 1F
2 Chome 46-5 Kanda Jinbōchō, Chiyoda-ku, Tokyo-to

Open
4:00pm-12:00am
Closed
Sunday
Tel. 03-3263-2008

Direction
Get out of Subway Jimbocho Station A4 exit and turn left at Hakusan Street towards Suidobashi direction. At the second signal, turn left at the corner of pork cutlet shop. Located immediately to the left side. 8 minutes walk

Speaking of Jinbocho, it is known as Tokyo's center of used-book stores and publishing houses. However, there are also many long-established eateries in business here. Among them is a Yakiton place with an open deck and den at the entrance.

Nevertheless, the atmosphere here is like a cafe rather than a grilled chicken place. This is because apparently it was originally a bistro. When the owner took over the business, the interior stayed the same. No wondered it looks western.

A place like this would be easy for foreign tourist to stop by. By the way it was just opened in April 2015. When inside, you will notice the blackboards with the menu written are everywhere. The biggest blackboard found in the back has a picture of a pig with descriptions of different cuts parts.

Due to its location, this place gets filled with officer workers who come for a quick drink between 7 and 9 pm. In the hot summer season, it's fantastic to go out the deck and enjoy the cool breeze and beer.

新橋やきとん
神田神保町店

神田神保町　　焼きトン

　神保町といえば、古書店街として有名だが、実は老舗の飲食店も多く営業している。そんな中、ここは入口玄関にデーンとオープンデッキがある、開放的な焼きとん屋さんだ。

　それにしても、焼きとん屋さんというよりカフェみたいな雰囲気の店内。聞けば元々はビストロだったところを、ほぼ居抜きで営業しているからだとか。なるほど納得。

　ここなら外国の観光客も入りやすそう。ちなみにオープンは何と2015年の4月というから新店なのだ。まず目に付くのが、店内随所にある黒板に書かれたメニュー。奥の一番大きいのには豚の絵に、それぞれ部位の説明なんかも書かれている。

　場所柄、夜7時から9時はサラリーマンで一杯になるんだとか。夏の季節は表のデッキに出て風に当たりながらジョッキを上げるのが最高だ。

東京都千代田区神田神保町2-46-5 ハローレジデンス神保町1階

営　午前4時から夜12時まで
休　日曜日
TEL　03-3263-2008

アクセス
地下鉄神保町駅A4出口を出て白山通りを左へ、水道橋方面へ進み、2つ目の信号のトンカツ屋さんの角を左へ曲がってスグ左側。徒歩8分。

02 Yakitorisho Tasuku

Kanda   **Yakitori**

Kanda Station is the battleground for Izakaya restaurants. This Japanese style pub is located very near the station and easy to recognize. Once you enter, there are tables and a counter with chicken grilling right behind it. The room is filled with the smell of smoke from the sizzling chicken.

Seats are taken by office workers as soon as it opens. Counters are also quickly filled with who seems to be frequent regulars. The menu is written on the big school blackboard indicating today's special and recommendations. Besides skewered chicken, there are fried items, fish and a substantial side menu to choose from. The restaurant has a second floor with a capacity of 40 people total. If you are looking for a casual and pleasant restaurant to taste the true Japanese style Yakitori, this is definitely the place to go.

---

3 Chome 22-11 Uchikanda Chiyoda-ku, Tokyo-to

Open
3:00pm-The first train next morning

Closed
Never Closed. Open throughout the year

Tel. 03-3253-2033

Direction
Exit at JR Kanda Station north exit. Go pass through the building that has the revolving sushi bar in front of you. After passing through the building, It will be located right diagonally forward.

やきとり将　タスク

神田　　焼き鳥

神田駅周辺といえば、居酒屋激戦区でどこも盛況です。そんな中、駅近くで一際目立つ店構えの焼き鳥屋さんが同店です。入れば手前にテーブル、奥にカウンターでその中で煙をモクモクさせて焼鳥が焼かれています。

開店と同時にもぉ仕事帰りのサラリーマン客で席が埋まっていきます。あっという間にカウンターは常連さんらしき客がズラリと並びます。

メニューはというと、学校の教室の並に大きい黒板に本日のオススメがいっぱい書かれています。焼鳥以外にフライものもあるし、魚もあって焼き鳥以外のサイドメニューも充実しています。客席は２階にもあって、全部で40人は入れます。お手軽に日本の焼き鳥屋の雰囲気を味わうには打って付けな店なのです。

東京都千代田区内神田3-22-11

営　午後３時から翌朝始発まで
休　年中無休
TEL　03-3253-2033

アクセス
ＪＲ神田駅北口を出て、スグ目の前にある回転寿司の入っているビルの中を通り抜けた右斜め前。

03 Taishū kappō Chirihama

Nihonbashi **Kaisen Izakaya**

Nihonbashi is a popular town close to Otemachi and Kanda. Modern office complexes are built among long-established eateries. It is a city for sophisticated adults.

Among those is the restaurant called Chirihama which features seafood, especially fresh fish. Traditional wood wall at the store front. Inside is bright and clean. Table and counter seating with a capacity of 20 people. Primary customers are middle-aged office workers. Young female office workers also come during lunch for their fresh fish platters.

A good look inside and you will be amazed at the abundance of the menus. Fresh sashimi and variety of fish to choose from. One of their specialties is the exotic Fugu-puffer fish hot pot. This will make a perfect dating spot or a great choice for business lunch and dinners. You can dine with a peace of mind that everyone will be satisfied here.

Nihonbashi Asahi Building 1F
4 Chome 1-14 Chuo-ku, Nihonbashi-muromachi Tokyo-to

Open
11:30pm-2:00am
5:00pm-11:00pm

Closed
Sunday & Holidays

Tel. 03-3277-2310

Direction
Take the JR Kanda Station south exit. After crossing the intersection, enter the Nichigin Street and turn left at the third crossroads. Turn right at the first corner and it will be located to your immediate right.

大衆割烹　千里濱

【日本橋】　【海鮮居酒屋】

　このあたり、神田でも大手町にも近い日本橋は室町。オフィスビルの間に古くからある老舗の飲食店が建ち並ぶ、いわゆる大人の街です。

　そんな中、白木の壁が映える店構えが特徴のお店です。明るくて清潔感溢れる店内で、カウンターとテーブルが並んでいてキャパは20人くらいです。客層は明らかに中高年のサラリーマンでランチとなると魚好きなOLも訪れるとのことです。

　まず店内を見回すと、短冊や黒板のメニューのその豊富さにビックリします。魚の新鮮さがウリでお刺身はモチロンあらゆる美味しいところが頂けます。

　フグ鍋も刺しも頂けるからここならリッチなデートでも、ちょいとした接待でも使える。そんな安心感のある本格的な大人の居酒屋さんといえます。

東京都中央区日本橋室町4-1-14
日本橋アサヒビル1階

営　午前11時30分から午前2時、夕方5時から11時まで
休　日曜日・祝日
TEL　03-3277-2310

アクセス
JR神田駅南口を出て、交差点を渡って日銀通りに入り、3つ目の十字路を左に入って最初の角を右に曲がってスグ右側。

04 Tatsumiya

Kudanshita **Sushi & Kaisen Izakaya**

Although Kudanshita is a place where a lot of office buildings are located, you will find varieties of eateries on the first floor of the buildings.

Located in front of Senshu University, Tatsumiya is a clean and elegant Japanese sushi and seafood restaurant. There are two entrance doors. The left sliding door takes you to the counter section and the right one takes you to the table section. All connected in one big space which can seat up to 30 people.

Fresh sashimi is stored inside the glass case. Sushi is made fresh as you order. Customers are mainly office workers. However, the recent establishment of the business hotels nearby has brought customers who are traveling on business trips. Open during lunch. The recommendation is the Tuna Bowl.

3 Chome 1-3 Nishikanda Chiyoda-ku, Tokyo-to

Open
5:00pm-11:00pm

Closed
Saturday, Sunday and Holidays

Tel. 03-3264-6656

Direction
Exit from subway Kudanshita Station and head toward Jimbocho direction at Yasukuni Street. Go under the freeway's overhead structure and turn left at Senshu University intersection. At the first crossroad make another left and it will be located immediately to the right. Right in front of Senshu University.

辰巳家

| 九段下 | 寿司＆海鮮居酒屋 |

　このあたりはオフィスビルの多い所だけど、ポツポツとビルのテナント１階には様々な飲食店が営業しています。

　そんな中、上品な清潔感溢れる店構えの店を見つけました。入口が２つあって、左側の屋号の書かれた暖簾を潜って中へ。なるほどこちらはカウンター席で、もう一つの入口を入るとテーブル席ですが、実は中で繋がっているのでした。客席は全部で30席といったところです。

　カウンターにはガラスケースがあって、寿司ネタが並んでいて本格的な寿司もつまめます。お客さんは場所柄ほとんどがサラリーマン。それも最近周辺にビジネスホテルが建ちだした影響で、出張族の御用達にもなっているようです。昼間はランチもやっていて中でも鉄火丼はオススメです。

東京都千代田区西神田3-1-3

営 夕方5時から11時まで
休 土・日・祝日
TEL 03-3264-6656

アクセス
地下鉄九段下駅を出て、靖国通りを神保町方面へ。高速の高架を潜って専修大学前交差点を左に曲がり、最初の十字路を更に左に曲がったスグ右。専修大学の真ん前。

05 Robata

Akihabara **Izakaya**

It's Akihabara, the Holy Land of the geek. Recently, area around here has undergone a constant redevelopment. Many high raised buildings are built in front of the station which has transformed Akihabara into an urbanized modern city.

Meanwhile, a few blocks from the station is a restaurant called Robata. The appearance remains Showa, a bit mismatch from its surroundings.

There are tables and counter seats that go around the kitchen in the first floor. If you go up the second floor, you will find yourself in a tatami mat parlor, full of Japanese essence.

Lately, more and more foreign tourists have been coming to this place. Their menu includes tempura and sashimi which are favorites among foreigners. Here, one can taste and experience Japanese food without much formality.

3 Chome 11-11 Sotokanda Chiyoda-ku, Tokyo-to

Open
11:00am-3:00pm
5:00pm-11:00pm
(weekends and holidays 11:00am-8:30pm)

Closed
Open throughout the year

Tel. 03-3253-6030

Direction
Exit from the Akihabara Electric Town exit at JR Akihabara Station. Turn right at Central Main Street. Then turn to the left at Kanda Shrine Street intersection. Located immediately to the left after turning right at the corner where there is a convenience store to the right.

炉ばた

秋葉原　居酒屋

オタクの聖地と呼ばれている秋葉原だけど、いやはや再開発が凄まじくて、知らぬ間に駅前には高層ビルが建ち、ますます未来都市化が進行しているようです。

そんな中、駅からしばらく歩いた路地にあるのが昭和の佇まいの同店。正にブレードランナー的ミスマッチ感。

1階は厨房を囲むカウンターとテーブル席もありますが、2階の畳敷きのお座敷に上がれば、一気に日本情緒が漂います。

最近は場所柄だけに外国人観光客も暖簾を潜ることも多いとか。それだけに外国人好みな天ぷらと刺身を一緒に味わえるメニューなども用意されているため気軽に和食体験ができるのでした。

東京都千代田区外神田3-11-11

営 午前11時から3時。夕方5時から11時まで。土日祝11時から8時30分
休 年中無休
TEL 03-3253-6030

アクセス
JR秋葉原駅の電気街口を出て中央大通りを右へ進み、神田明神通り交差点を左へ曲がり、右側にあるコンビニの角を右へ入ったスグ左側。

06 KIRIKA

Uguisudani **Snack Izakaya**

Uguisudani is a place where traditional downtown feels still exit. On a quiet corner, there is a western café bar called Kirika. Once you enter, surprisingly this place is packed with customers. Young male customers come here one after another. There is a counter and tables which fit 17 people altogether.

Playing disco music in the background, you can sing karaoke as well. It's a combination of a snack bar and Izakaya.

Customers are mainly middle-aged and young office workers. Run by a beautiful mama-san, named KIRIKA. She manages this whole place all by herself. A friendly spot for people who want to experience shitamachi downtown in modern Japan.

---

5 Chome 11-3
Higashinippori
Arakawa-ku, Tokyo-to

Open
10:00am-12:00am
(10:00 to 0:00)

Closed
Sunday and Holidays

Tel. 03-6806-8891

Direction
Exit at JR Uguisudani Station north exit. Cross the signal at Kototoi bashi Street and enter Otakebashi Street. After passing the elementary school, turn left at the corner of the liquor store. 7 minutes walk

KIRIKA

| 鶯谷 | スナック居酒屋 |

　このあたりは東京の下町風情が漂うエリアです。そんな一角にあるのが洋風のカフェバー風居酒屋なのです。中に入ってビックリ！　何とお客でギッシリ。それでも次から次へと若い男性の1人客がやってきます。入って手前のカウンターと奥のテーブル席でざっと17人が限界といったところ。

　ＢＧＭは80年代の懐かしいディスコミュージックが流れております。カラオケも歌えるというから、スナックと居酒屋が一緒になったような感じです。

　客層は中高年に若いサラリーマンといったところ。サバサバとして、気取らない下町の美人ママは店名そのままＫＩＲＩＫＡさん。こんな忙しい店なのにママ1人で切り盛りしている。日本の現在の下町体験をするのに打って付けなフランクな店なのです。

東京都荒川区東日暮里5-11-3

営 午前10時から夜12時
休 日曜日・祝日
Tel 03-6806-8891

アクセス
ＪＲ鶯谷駅北口を出て、言問橋通りの信号を渡って尾竹橋通りへ入り、小学校の前を過ぎて二筋目、酒屋の角を左に曲がってスグ右側。徒歩7分。

07 Ebi Kani-ya

Kitasenju **Ebi & Kani Senmon Izakaya**

Since the old day, Kitasenju has been "the town" with many drinking places. Located at the famous Nomiya Yokocho which means Bar-Street is this shrimp and crab specialty Izakaya called Ebi Kani-ya. A restaurant which is easy to miss. With a tiny entrance, first floor has a counter that sits 7 or 8 people, and the second floor has tables. With a total capacity of 22, it's big enough for groups.

A look at the menu on the wall, you will notice everything is associated with shrimp or crab. Even the appetizer is something made from shrimp. AND to make washing hands easy, automatic faucet is installed at the counter in front of each seat.

Owner opened this place because he loves shrimp. His obsession with shrimp is clearly demonstrated here. This is no doubt a place for shrimp and crab lovers.

Koizumi building 1F
2 Chome 65 Kitasenju, Adachi-ku, Tokyo-to

Open 5:30pm-11:30pm
Closed Sunday
Tel. 03-5284-9630

Direction
Exit at JR Kitasenju Station west exit and turn left after passing McDonalds. You will enter a bar alley. Walk the alley for about 50 meters and it will be located to the left. 6 minutes walk

えびかに家

北千住 **エビ&カニ専門居酒屋**

　この北千住という町も昔っから飲み屋さんがいっぱいあるTHE下町です。そんな中、飲み屋街として有名な「飲み屋横丁」の中程にあるのがこのエビカニ専門店。

　思わず通り過ぎてしまうほどに間口が小さい入口のドアを開けて中に入ると、ざっと7〜8席座れるカウンターがあり2階にもテーブル席があって全部で22席余りだからグループ客もOKです。

　壁に貼られているメニューを見るとこれがエビ、エビ、カニばかりです。カウンターに腰掛けて前を見ると、何と手洗い用の自動水洗の蛇口があって手掴みでムシャムシャと頂く方式なのです。お通しも、海老の練り物なんかが出てきて、海老に徹底的にこだわっています。御店主の海老好きが高じてオープンさせた同店。いやはや珍しい店なのです。

東京都足立区北千住2-65　小泉ビル1階

営　夕方5時から11時30分
休　日曜日
TEL　03-5284-9630

アクセス
JR北千住駅西口を出て、マクドナルドの先を左に曲がるとある飲み屋路地の通称「飲み屋横丁」に入って50メートル程いった左側。徒歩6分。

08 Tsukiji Fuku

`Tsukiji` `Izakaya`

This Izakaya is located behind the Tsukiji Honganji Temple, on a small street between two buildings, a place difficult to find for people who come here for the first time. Look for the white electric signboard with the word "fuku" written on it. As you open the snack style wooden door, there is an 8 seat counter and an 8 seat table. A cozy casual home cooking restaurant with calm and chic atmosphere.

The menu includes seasonal homemade dishes and fish. Their fish comes from the same Tsukiji wholesaler as the famous sushi restaurant where President Obama ate. Because the restaurant is picky on what they serve, they buy only the freshest fish so their food always tastes great. A popular hidden treasure for the local retirees and office workers.

---

7 Chome 11-11
Tsukiji Chuo-ku,
Tokyo-to

Open
11:00am-2:00pm
(lunchtime)
6:00pm-11:00pm

Closed
Saturday, Sunday and Holidays

Tel. 03-6278-8125

Direction
From Tsukiji Honganji Temple intersection, enter the road on the side of Honganji Temple. After crossing Tsukiji 7-chome intersection, enter the narrow street between Bento shop and Tempura shop that has an iron barred door.

築地ふく

築地　　居酒屋

　場所が築地本願寺の裏手あたりのちょうどビルとビルの間の通用口みたいな路地を入った所にあってビックリさせられます。これは初めて来た人はまず解らない立地です。

　渋い白の電灯看板にはふくと書かれています。スナック風のドアを開けて入ると、中は白木のカウンターに8席とテーブル席8席の和風。小料理屋といった風情です。大人が落ち着いて飲める店です。

　メニューは四季折々の日本の家庭料理を基本として、あのオバマ大統領も食べた銀座の有名寿司店にもネタを卸している築地市場の問屋から、通を唸らせる新鮮なネタを仕入れている為、本当に美味しい魚も頂けます。それだけに味にうるさい近所のご隠居や会社のサラリーマンたちに人気の店なのです。

東京都中央区築地7-11-11

営 午前11時から2時（ランチ）。夕方6時から11時まで
休 土日祝日
TEL 03-6278-8125

アクセス
築地本願寺交差点から、本願寺脇の道を入って真っ直ぐ歩いて、築地七丁目交差点を渡って弁当屋と天ぷら屋さんの間の鉄格子の扉のある細い路地に入ってスグ。

09 Motsu Masa

Asakusa **Yakiton**

This is a long established Yakiton eatery. You might hesitate to go in at first from the look outside. A counter only eatery which sits roughly 10. Right above the counter are the old-fashioned wooden menu plates. You can definitely feel the history here.

A family run business currently managed by the mother and the son. The original owner who started this placed was trained in a traditional Japanese cuisine restaurant. It's been 14 years since the restaurant was taken over by his heir.

Customers ranging from regulars, neighborhood restaurant owners to second generation peers and office workers who are here on business. They fill up this place as soon as it opens so it is recommended to go at early hours.

Opposed to the tourist place, you can experience a different Asakusa here.

2 Chome 1-8 Nishiasakusa Taito-ku, Tokyo-to

Open 5:00pm-12:00am
Closed Sunday
Tel. 03-3841-9617

Direction
From Asakusa Subway Station, turn right at International Street. Located on the left after turning left at the first alley.

もつ政

浅草　　焼きトン

　昔っからある老舗の焼きトン屋さんです。初めてだとちょいと入りづらい感じの店構えかもしれません。店内はカウンターだけでザッと10人は座れそうです。カウンターの上を見ると「舌代」と書いて（しながき）と読ませる古風で渋いメニューの木札がぶら下がってたりして、老舗の雰囲気が漂います。

　厨房では2代目とお母さんの2人が切り盛りしています。先代のお父さんは元々和食の割烹料理のお店で修行した職人気質の方だったそうで、2代目が店を継いで14年目になるとのことです。

　客筋は古くから来ている常連さんや、地元浅草の同業者、それも同じ2代目仲間や、出張で来ているサラリーマン客がほとんどで開店と同時に押し寄せてスグに席は埋まりますから早い時間がオススメです。観光地とは違う浅草の下町風情を体験することのできる名店なのです。

東京都台東区西浅草2-1-8

営　夕方5時から夜12まで
休　日曜日
TEL　03-3841-9617

アクセス
地下鉄浅草駅から雷門通りを国際通りに出て右へ。1つ目の路地を左に入って左側。

10 Tsukiji Tabechaina Tabenbaru

Tsukiji　**Chūka izakaya**

Around Tsukiji Honganji temple, there is a variety of old and new Japanese restaurants. However, there is only one Chinese food Izakaya serving Schzechuan cuisine. The decoration does not look Chinese but rather a western café. Menus are not limited to Chinese food also. There are sashimi and other Japanese dishes. It has a capacity of roughly 20 with both counter and table seating. The chef who works here used to work at Holiday Inn. A real cook with years of experience. The food tastes great and the prices aren't too expensive. Daily lunch specials and other services are available.

7 Chome 16-9 Tsukiji Chuo-ku, Tokyo-to

Open
11:30am-2:00pm
5:00pm-12:00am
(Saturday, Sunday, and Holidays from 4:00pm-11:30pm)

Closed
Open throughout the year

Tel. 03-3543-2966

Direction
Enter Tsukiji Honganji Temple intersection from subway Tsukiji Station. Walk the road beside Honganji Temple towards the direction of Sumida River and turn right at the end of the road. Located at the corner of the third block after turning left at the first corner.

築地たべチャイナ・たべんばる

`築地`　`中華居酒屋`

築地本願寺周辺には、和食系を中心とした新旧様々な飲食店が営業していますが四川料理の中華居酒屋はここだけです。

店内を見渡せば中華屋さんらしくない洋風カフェみたいで女の子が喜ぶような内装なのです。でもメニューは中華だけじゃなくて、刺身もあるしちゃんと和食メニューも並んでいます。

店内はカウンターとテーブルと小上がりもあってだいたい20人のキャパです。厨房で腕を振るうのは元ホリデー・インのコック長を務めたオーナーシェフを始め腕のいい本格的なコック達です。なのに嬉しいのが値段の安さ。日替わりで様々な特典サービスも実施しています。

東京都中央区築地7-16-9

営 午前11時30分から午後2時。夕方5時から深夜12時まで。土日祝は夕方4時から11時30分（ランチ休み）
休 年中無休
TEL 03-3543-2966

アクセス
地下鉄築地駅から築地本願寺交差点に出て、本願寺横を真っ直ぐ墨田川方面へ入り突き当たりを右へ曲がって、最初の角を左に入って3筋目の角。徒歩7分。

11 Kisui Gochitama

Suidobashi **Izakaya**

Many unique Izakaya have been built around Suidobashi. Kisui Gochitama is a brand new Izakaya that opened last September. Serving lunch, this place is visited by customers of various ages from students to office workers.

Once inside, you will hear a loud and cheerful greeting from the staffs. All the workers are men. Some have beard which make them look wild. Some are big which make them look ferocious like professional wrestlers. Despite their looks, they make delicious and delicate Japanese food, which you might find it hard to believe.

For your information, their menu includes fish, yakitori, and other dishes. This place gets busy by 7pm. If you are going with a group, it is recommended to get there early or make a reservation.

2 Chome 13-6 Misakicho Chiyoda-ku, Tokyo-to

Open
11:30am-2:00pm
5:00pm-11:00pm
Closed
Sunday
Tel. 03-3556-5266

Direction
Take the JR Suidobashi west exit and turn left. Then turn left at the fifth intersection before the gas station. Located on the right side.

季酔・ごち魂

| 水道橋 | 居酒屋 |

　この水道橋近辺には個性的な居酒屋さんがけっこう建ち並んでいます。そんな中、昨年9月にオープンした新店です。昼間はランチもやっていて、学生からサラリーマンまで様々な年齢層の客が訪れるとのことです。

　中に入ると、野太い男性の声がして、なるほど活気みなぎっています。店員さんは全員男性で、しかも髭を蓄えていて貫禄充分なワイルドな雰囲気。どう見ても獰猛なプロレスラーって感じだけど、なかなか繊細な和食の肴が頂けてそのギャップが面白い。因みにメニューは魚や焼き鳥もあって種類は豊富です。

　特に夜7時頃になると混み出すという同店。グループ客ならなるべく早めに入るのが望ましいかもしれません。

東京都千代田区三崎町2-13-6

営 午前11時30分から2時。夕方5時から夜11時まで
休 日曜日
TEL 03-3556-5266

アクセス
JR水道橋西口を出て、左へ進んで5筋目のガソリンスタンド手前を左へ入ってしばらく歩いた右側。

12 Izakaya Yakyū Kozō

Nihonbashi **Izakaya**

Speaking of Nihonbashi, close to Ginza, is a place where many companies' headquarter office is located. There are also a lot of long-established eateries and sweets shops here from the Edo period. Among such, there is a little Izakaya with an unusual name "Yakyu Kozo" which means "Baseball Boy".

If you go down the stairs to the basement you will find yourself inside a modern Japanese-style accent restaurant in creamy white wood, very different from the atmosphere outside. This place offers mainly Japanese dish and pub menus. Uniforms of professional baseball teams, player's signatures, and posters are decorated on the walls. As a bonus, there is a baseball game board on the counter. You can also watch baseball match live on their large TV monitor. Just like its name, this is a place where baseball fans gather. Carp fan girls whom are trending in Japan also show up here.

Kimeta Housing 20th building Underground 1F
1 Chome 10-2 Nihonbashihonchō Chuo-ku, Tokyo-to

Open
Monday to Friday
11:00am-2:30pm
Monday to Saturday
5:00pm-11:00pm

Closed
Sunday and Holidays

Tel. 03-6262-3597

Direction
Turn right to Ningyocho directon after exiting from Subway Ginza line, Mitsukoshimae Station B6 exit. Located immediately to the right after crossing the Edobashi North intersection.

居酒屋　野球小僧

| 日本橋 | 居酒屋 |

　日本橋といえば銀座にも近く様々な企業の本社ビルが立ち並ぶオフィスビル街ですが、江戸の昔からやっている老舗の飲食店や和菓子屋を多く見かけます。そんな中に、ちょっと珍しい店名の居酒屋さんを見つけました。その名も「野球小僧」。

　地下へ階段を降りて行くと外の雰囲気とうって変わって落ち着いた白木のカウンターがアクセントになっている和風な店内です。和食を中心に居酒屋メニューも楽しめるところです。壁にはプロ野球チームのユニホームが飾ってさり気なく選手のサインボールもあります。おまけにカウンターの隅には野球ゲーム盤が置いて、大型モニターでは専門チャンネルで野球中継も見られます。店名通り野球好きが集まる店なのです。今流行りのカープ女子も出没するらしいです。

東京都中央区日本橋本町1-10-2
きめたハウジング
第20ビル地下1階

営 午前11時から午後2時30分（月曜日から金曜日）夕方5時から11時まで（月曜日から土曜日）

休 日曜日・祝日
TEL 03-6262-3597

アクセス
地下鉄銀座線、三越前駅Ｂ６出口を出て右へ人形町方面へ。江戸橋北交差点を渡ってスグ右側。

Sennen Soba Asakusa Tawaramachiten

13

Asakusa **Soba Izakaya**

Deviated from the tourist attraction, Kaminarimon, towards Tawaramachi direction. Sobanomidokoro is an easy to enter and casual Soba chain located near Tawaramachi Station. Inexpensive too. Soba starting at a price of 260 yen. Both counter and table seats are available for up to 20 people. By the way, among the chain locations, only the ones in the Asakusa vicinity serve alcohol. You will notice many customers drinking from early hours.

This place turns into an Izakaya from evening. Photos of the menus are put up on the wall like a cafeteria which makes it easy to see what to order. A poster says "No-smoking between 11:00 to 2pm" is also found. Smoking is allowed in the evening hours. Recently many foreign guests who are staying at the nearby hotels are seen here as well.

1 Chome 7-20 Nishiasakusa Taito-ku, Tokyo-to

Open
24 hours a day
Closed
Open throughout the year
Tel. 03-3847-8300

Direction
Walk from Asakusa Kaminarimon Street into Kokusai Street. Cross the signal and turn left. Located next to the pharmacy.

せんねんそば
浅草田原町店

浅草　　蕎麦居酒屋

　観光客でごったがえす雷門前から外れた田原町方面へ。田原町駅近くに「そば飲み処」なんて書いてある気楽に入れるチェーン店の蕎麦屋です。なにしろかけが260円。でも中に入るとカウンターにテーブル席があって全部で20人は入れます。因みに酒が飲めるのはこの同じ店の系列店でも浅草地区だけ。見ればお客さんたちみんな早い時間からグビグビやってます。

　当然夕方からは居酒屋状態になるとのこと。壁にはつまみや料理の写真メニューが、食堂みたいに貼ってあります。

　張り紙の中に「禁煙タイムは午前11時〜14時」とあって夕方からは喫煙できます。最近は近くのホテルに泊まってる外国人観光客もよく顔を出すそうです。

東京都台東区西浅草1-7-20

営 24時間営業
休 年中無休
TEL 03-3847-8300

アクセス
浅草雷門通りから国際通りへ突き当たって、信号を渡り左へしばらく歩いたところ薬局の隣り。

14　Kō-Chan

Tawaramachi　**Izakaya**

A new spot for foreign tourists. Tawaramachi Station, the closest station to the tool shop street near Kappa Bridge. A little away from Asakusa with Higashi Honganji Temple and Buddhist altar shops nearby. Kō-Chan is located right by the major intersection. From its appearance, it looks like a casual eatery. Many menus written on the short strips of papers are found on the wall. Authentic oriental herbals hot pot for 1,598 yen, Chinese style dishes, noodles, fried items and even sashimi. This place is like an Asian cafeteria.

And prices are cheap too. On a rainy day, drinks are from 162 yen. If you pay one thousand yen, you can get pretty drunk. Round tables, with a capacity of about 20 to 30 people. It's a good spot to relax during the daytime hour. Customers are mainly office workers, locals and the retired people from the neighborhood.

Happō building 1F 1 Chome 2-2 Nishiasakusa Taito-ku, Tokyo-to

Open
11:00am-2:00pm
4:30pm-11:00pm
(Saturday, Sunday, and Holidays from noon-11:00pm)

Closed
Open throughout the year

Tel. 03-5827-1195

Direction
Get off at Asakusa Subway Tawaramachi Station. Go from Kotobuki 4-chome intersection into Asakusa Street towards the Ueno direction. Located shortly after passing the post office. 1 minute walk

こ〜ちゃん

| 田原町 | 居酒屋 |

　外国人観光客などでごった返している浅草から少し離れた田原町駅は、かっぱ橋道具屋街の最寄り駅。近くには東本願寺などがあり仏壇仏具のお店が目立ちます。そんな大通りの交差点近くにあるのが同店。いかにも大衆居酒場といった佇まい。まず目につくのは壁中に貼られたメニューの短冊です。本格的な薬膳火鍋（1598円）みたいな中華から、揚げ物にご飯物に麺類、それに刺身と、まさにアジアの大衆食堂といったラインナップなのです。

　しかも値段が安い。特に雨の日はサワー類が（162円）になるから千ベロ（千円でベロベロに酔える）の店と言えます。丸テーブルが並んでいて、キャパは20人〜30人ほど。早い時間だとマッタリ過ごせる穴場かもしれない。客層は昼間はサラリーマンやご近所のご隠居さんと地元の人ばかりです。

東京都台東区西浅草1-2-2　八宝ビル1階

営 午前11時から2時、夕方4時30分から夜11時（土、日、祝は昼12時から夜11時まで）
休 年中無休
Tel 03-5827-1195

[アクセス]
地下鉄浅草線は田原町駅を上がって、寿四丁目交差点に出て、浅草通りを上野方面へ。郵便局を過ぎてスグ。徒歩1分。

West Area
西部地区

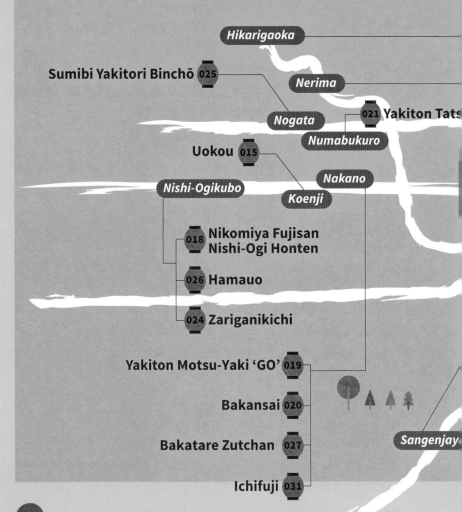

Nerima-ku （練馬区）
Nakano-ku （中野区）
Suginami-ku （杉並区）
Setagaya-ku （世田谷区）

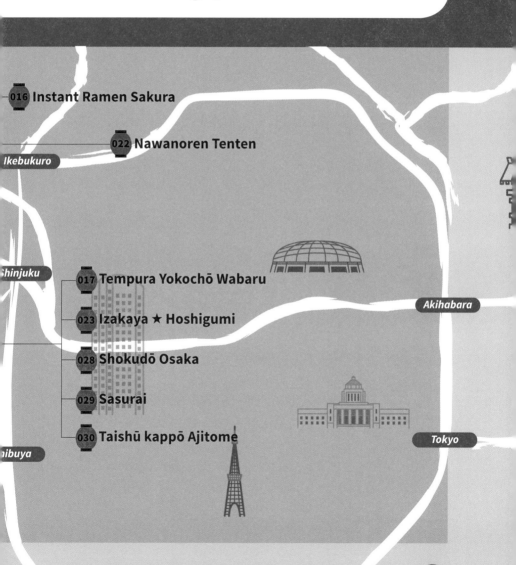

15 Uokou

Koenji **Seafood Izakaya**

There are many kinds of Izakaya, Japanese style pub, in the city Koenji but this particular one is also a fish shop.

There is an L-shaped counter to the left and table seating is arranged in the right side against the wall. It can accommodate 30 people comfortably. On the second floor, there is private room. This room is by reservation only and is used for special events such as traditional Japanese storytelling, known as Rakugo, and banquets.

According to the owner, this place was a fish shop originally. It has been in business for more than 30 years. Currently, half of the store space is used for Izakaya and the other half remains as fish shop.

The Izakaya section is 18 years old and run by Tsurumi Matsui and her husband. Uokou is an at-home Izakaya where customers are greeted with warm hospitality and humorous conversations.

2 Chome 22-8
Kōenjikita
Suginami-ku,
Tokyo-to

Open
4:00pm-11:00pm
Closed
Monday
Tel. 03-3339-5778

Direction
Exit at JR Koenji Station south exit. Enter the Junjo shopping street in front of you and turn left at the end of the street, entering the Koshin Street shopping district. Make an immediate right and it will be located on the right-hand side.

うおこう

高円寺 **海鮮居酒屋**

　高円寺にも色んな居酒屋さんがありますが中でも魚屋さんがやっているお店がここです。店内は左にＬ字のカウンターがあって、右側にテーブル席が並ぶ。広々としていて30人は座れそう。聞けば2階にお座敷もあるらしく、落語会なんかのイベントや、宴会の時だけ開けているとか。

　元々は30年前から続く老舗の魚屋さんだったそうで、店舗を半分居酒屋にして、今も並行して営業しているそうです。

　ちなみに居酒屋の方は18年目。奥の厨房で腕を振るうシャイなご主人と女将の松井つるみさんのお2人で切り盛りしています。

　軽妙な語り口で接客するチャーミングな女将さんのいるアットホームな居酒屋なのです。

東京都杉並区高円寺北2-22-8

営　夕方4時から11時まで
休　月曜日
TEL　03-3339-5778

[アクセス]
ＪＲ高円寺駅は南口を出て、目の前にある純情商店街に入り、突き当たりを左へ曲がって庚申通り商店街に出て右に曲がるとスグ右側。

16 Instant Ramen Sakura

Nerima Hikarigaoka   **Instant Ramen Izakaya**

This unique Japanese instant noodle shop is located along the busy national highway. It is unusual to find an Izakaya near Hikarigaoka vicinity where high-rise housing complexes are abundant.

When you open the wooden door and go inside, you will see counters and tables that sit roughly 20 people. Immediately, you will notice the multiple shelves on the walls. An amazing collection of instant ramen from all over Japan, from the most northern prefecture Hokkaido to the southernmost prefecture Okinawa. A partial collection from what is now more than 10,000 kinds nationwide. No wonder it is fun to come here. When you find an instant noodle that appeals to you, you can either purchase it and bring it home or have them cook it right there on the spot. Guaranteed you will be impressed by the great taste of the noodles that will make you doubt it's instant. This is definitely a unique Izakaya where one can experience and enjoy Japan's advanced food processing technology first hand.

Emerald building
1F 5 Chome
7-10 Nerima-ku,
Takamatsu,
Tokyo-to

Open
11:30am-2:00pm
5:30pm-11:00pm
Closed
Sunday & Holidays
Tel. 03-6794-6777

Direction
Using Subway Oedo Line, get off at Hikarigaoka Station. From the station main street, turn to the left at 6-chome intersection of Sasame Street. Destination at the sequence of Cadenza Hotel next to Ramen shop. 10 minutes walk

ラーメン甲子園
居酒屋さくら

練馬光が丘　インスタントラーメン居酒屋

車の流れが激しい国道沿いにこの店はあります。高層団地が立ち並ぶ、盛り場のない光が丘近辺では珍しい居酒屋です。バーのような木のドアを開けて中に入ると、カウンターとテーブル席があって、ざっと20人は座れます。

まずは壁にある棚を見て驚かされます。北は北海道から南は沖縄まで、全国のインスタントラーメンがズラ〜リと展示されているからです。現在全国に1万種近く作られているというインスタント袋麺のほんの一部ですが、当然その中から好きなのを選んで調理もしてくれます。しかもどれを食べてももはやインスタントを超えた旨さにさらに驚かされます。日本の食品加工技術のすばらしさを堪能できるちょっと変わった居酒屋なのです。

東京都練馬区高松5-7-10
エメラルドビル1階

営　昼11時30分から午後2時。夕方5時30分から11時まで
休　日曜日・祝日
TEL　03-6794-6777

アクセス
地下鉄大江戸線光が丘駅。駅前大通りから笹目通りの6丁目交差点を左へ。「ホテル・カデンツァ」の並び、ラーメン屋の隣り。徒歩10分。

17 Tempura Yokochō Wabaru

Sangenjaya **Tempura Izakaya**

Speaking of Sangenjaya, many people have heard of the famous Suzuran Street. A busy street with a diversity of eating places. In the middle of such a street is Izakaya, Wabaru, a restaurant specializing in Tempura. To find it, look for signs with "Tempura" written in the Hiragana. Once inside, a few steps up, table and counter seats are set up around the kitchen. Altogether 30 people can fit. Somehow, this place is full of Showa era vibe. During Edo period, Tempura was a daily staple for Japanese people treated like fast food, but today, tempura has turned into a popular high-end Japanese cuisine. With the intention of going back to the origin of Tempura, this place fries their Tempura on a skewer like in the Edo period. With easy one skewer order, you can try many dishes without breaking the bank.

Torii building 1F
4 Chome 22-13
Taishido, Setagaya-ku, Tokyo-to

Open
6:00pm-5:00am
Closed
Open throughout the year
Tel. 03-6805-5535

Direction
Find the police box at the Sangenjaya Station of the Denentoshi line. Enter the Suzuran Street located next to the police box. Destination at the left side of Suzuran Street.

てんぷら横町・わばる

`三軒茶屋`　　`天ぷら居酒屋`

　三軒茶屋といえばこちらの「すずらん通り」が盛り場として知られていますが、そんな通りの中程にあって「てんぷら」のひらがな文字が目印です。入ってスグのフロアーから、数段高くなる階段を上がって奥へ。手前にテーブル席が並んで、その奥は厨房を囲むように小さなカウンターがあります。全部で30人は入れそうな広さで店内は、何となく昭和を意識した雰囲気なのです。

　今や天ぷらは高級和食の定番となっていますが、実は江戸の昔は庶民のファストフードで串で揚げていたのでした。同店では今一度その天ぷら料理を庶民の手に取り戻すという思いを込めて串揚げにこだわっているんだとか。一串からの注文が可能で明朗会計でいたってリーズナブルなのが嬉しいのです。

東京都世田谷区太子堂4-22-13
鳥居ビル1F

営　夕方6時から翌朝5時まで
休　年中無休
TEL　03-6805-5535

[アクセス]
田園都市線は三軒茶屋駅近くの交番の脇を入った、すずらん通りの中、左側。

18 Nikomiya Fujisan Nishi-Ogi Honten

Nishi-Ogikubo **Stand and Drink Bar**

Nishi-Ogikubo has been the heart of standing pubs where foreign visitors and elderly locals are seen here and there. Nikomiya Fujisan, a newly opened Japanese standing pub is named after Mt. Fuji with the hope that it will be loved by a wide range of people just like Mt. Fuji.

Customers can choose smoking and non-smoking section when they come here. Non-smoking section is available until 11:00pm. When you enter the restaurant, don't be surprised to hear the sound of Taiko drums. A fun way of welcoming customers.

Their specialty stews are highly recommended. Two big pots contain red and white stews using red and white wine. The red stew is a bit sweet and rich while the white stew is salty and refreshing. If you order wine, you will be able to watch the performance of pouring wine from high above with spilling in the big pot. Beside stews, there is also whole roast chicken which is prepared on the spot.

---

3 Chome 25-6 Suginami-ku, Nishiogiminami, Tokyo-to

Open
6:00pm-2:00am (Saturday & Sunday starts at 12:00pm)

Closed
Open throughout the year

Tel. 070-6668-3426

Direction
It will be immediately to the right after turning right at the JR Nishi-Ogikubo Station south exit.

煮こみや　富士山
西荻本店

　西荻窪　　　立ち飲み

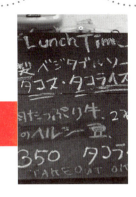

　最近は外国人観光客や、年配の散歩者もチラホラしている西荻窪で一番居酒屋が密集する路地の入口にある2015年の12月にオープンした立ち飲み屋です。店名の富士山は、裾の広い客層に愛されるようにという願いを込めてとのこと。

　店は左右にカウンターが分かれていて正面から見て右側が夜11時まで禁煙で左側が喫煙可能です。店内に入ると「ドンドン！」なんて太鼓を叩いて迎えてくれてビックリさせられます。

　ちなみにお店のオススメはシチューに似た煮込み。デンと置かれた2個の大鍋にはそれぞれ赤と白のワインを使った赤煮込みと白煮込みがあり、赤は甘みがあってこってり、白はさっぱり塩味。ワインを注文するとその大鍋の上でこぼしながら注ぐパフォーマンスもあったりして面白い。他にその場で鶏をローストするロースト丸鶏というのもあります。

東京都杉並区西荻窪3-25-6

営　夕方6時から深夜2時頃（土・日は昼12時から）
休　年中無休
Tel　070-6668-3426

アクセス
ＪＲ西荻窪駅南口を出て右へ入ってスグ右側。

19 Yakiton Motsu-Yaki 'GO'

Nakano **Motsu-Yaki**

Speaking of Nakano station, it is the Paradise for otaku people. It is also the Holy Land for middle-aged men who are looking for some fun.

On the north exit of the station, a little outside the busy district is a tiny restaurant called GO. A small place which holds only 8 people. Daily specials are written on the whiteboard on the wall such as fresh liver, tongue and other intestine sashimi.

The owner was trained at a famous kaiseki cuisine restaurant when he was young. A veteran chef with years of experience. No wonder this place feels long established even though it has only been open a few years. Hoppy Horoyoi value set is recommended. It comes with one glass of Hoppy drink and 5 different kinds of skewers.

2 Chome 7-12 Arai Nakano-ku, Tokyo-to

Open 5:00pm-12:00am
Closed Sunday
Tel. 03-3387-7425

Direction
Take the JR Nakano Station north exit. At Nakano Street, go towards Arai Yakushi direction. After passing the first intersection, it will be located to your left after walking for a while. Look for red lanterns. 7-8 minutes walk

やきとん・モツ焼き「豪」

中野　**モツ焼き**

　中野駅北口といえばオタクの聖地。でも大人のオヤジにとっては盛り場が充実している居酒屋の聖地でもあります。

　そんな北口の賑わいから少し外れた所に、ちょいと渋くあるのが同店。それこそ間口一間余りといった感じ。程良い狭さというか、カウンター8席だけの小さな店内です。奥に腰を降ろして、壁のホワイトボードのメニューを見ると、ホルモン系のお刺身も色々並んでいます。

　聞けばご主人は若い頃から懐石料理のお店で修行をみっちり積んだ職人さん。

　だからなのか、このお店はオープンしてまだ数年という新店なのに、老舗然とした落ち着きを醸し出しています。ホッピーに焼きトン5本ついて串1本お得な、ホッピーほろ酔いセットがオススメです。

東京都中野区新井2-7-12

営 夕方5時から24時
休 日曜日
TEL 03-3387-7425

アクセス
JR中野駅北口を出て、中野通りを新井薬師方面へ。最初の交差点を過ぎて、しばらく歩いた左側。数軒並ぶ店の1軒。赤提灯が目印。徒歩7~8分。

20 Bakansai

Nakano **Izakaya**

To find this restaurant, look for the signboard with big "BAKANSAI" written in Kanji characters. The word Bakan is referring to the area near the port of Shimonoseki in Yamaguchi Prefecture. Incidentally, the owner of this restaurant is from Yamaguchi Prefectures and that is why he named this place Bakansai. The owner is warm and easy going, so there is a good vive in the kitchen. Everyone seems to be enjoying working there.

Wrapped in warm lightings. Tables are in the front and counters are in the back. There is a second floor which is reserved for group banquets.

12 years in business. This is a well-known Izakaya in the Nakano neighborhood where people can drink until the late night. A wide variety of yakitori, fish and hot pot dishes are offered on the menu. The place also specializes horse meat sashimi and motsunabe also known as intestine hot pot.

2 Chome 29-7 Nakano Nakano-ku, Tokyo-to

Open
11:00am-2:00pm
6:00pm-2:00am
(Friday till 4:00am)

Closed
Once per month on Sunday

Tel. 03-5328-6139

Direction
Take the south exit of JR Nakano. Cross the rotary in front of you and walk along Nakano Street for about two minutes. Located on the left side

馬関彩
ばかんさい

`中野`　　`居酒屋`

目印は大きな「馬関彩」看板の文字です。この「馬関」は山口県の下関港一帯を言い表す昔からの言い方です。因みに店名の
由来はそのご主人が山口県出身の為。厨房にはホンワカしたそのご店主がいい味出していて、みんな楽しそうに働いている様子です。

暖色系の照明に包まれた店内は手前にテーブル席と奥にカウンター。2階もあって、そこはグループ客の貸し切り宴会のお座敷になっています。

すでに中野で12年も続いていて夜は遅くまで飲める居酒屋さんとして地元ではかなり有名なお店です。料理は焼き鳥から魚、鍋料理と幅広いのですがオススメは特製もつ鍋と馬刺しです。

東京都中野区中野
2-29-7

営 午前11時から2時（ランチタイム）。夕方6時から深夜2時。金曜日は早朝4時まで。
休 月に1度だけ日曜日がお休み（不定期）
TEL 03-5328-6139

アクセス
JR中野駅南口を出て目の前のロータリーを渡り、中野通りを2分程歩いた左側。

21 Yakiton Tatsuya

Numabukuro   **Yakiton**

Located at the residential area away from the shopping district of Numabukuro Station on the Seibu Shinjuku Line is a famous yakiton place called Tatsuya.

Big Yakiton written on the noren curtain, this place drifts with the Showa atmosphere.

All counters, roughly 27 seats. With a slight angle, you will see the faces of people sitting next to you. It's a place where people can easily chat and communicate with each other.

One unique characteristic of the Yakiton here is that it is grilled with miso sauce. Different from Shioyaki, which is grilled with salt, you can taste the miso flavor yakiton here. There is a public bathhouse nearby so many people stop by here after taking a bath.

---

3 Chome 27-6
Numabukuro
Nakano-ku, Tokyo-to

Open
5:00pm-11:00pm
(Sunday till 10:00pm)
Closed
Wednesday
Tel. 03-5942-9986

Direction
Exit at Numabukuro Station north exit using Seibu Shinjuku Line. Enter the shopping district to your right and turn to the left between bookstore and fruit shop at the second crossroad.

やきとん　たつや

`沼袋`　`焼きトン`

　西武新宿沿線の沼袋駅の商店街から外れた住宅街の中にぽつんとある有名店がここです。

　やきとん、と大きく書かれた暖簾を潜って硝子戸を開けて中へ入るとまさに昭和の風情が漂う店内です。

　客席はカウンターのみでざっと27席はあります。いわゆる真っ直ぐなカウンターじゃなくて微妙に角度が細かくついていて、自然と隣りの人の横顔を窺うことが出来て安心感もありコミュニケーションもとりやすいようになっています。

　ここの焼きトンは味噌ダレを付けて焼いているのが特徴で、塩焼きとはまた違った味噌の風味を楽しめます。近くには銭湯もあるし、湯上がりのお父さん達も訪れます。

東京都中野区沼袋3-27-6　1階

営 夕方5時から夜11時まで。日曜日は10時まで
休 水曜日
Tel 03-5942-9986

アクセス
西武新宿線沼袋駅北口を出て右の商店街に入り、2つ目の十字路にある書店と果物屋の間を左に曲がってスグ。

22 Nawanoren Tenten

Nerima **Stand and Drink Bar**

Geting off Nerima Station, Nawanoren Tenten is located at the north side business district. As soon as you step inside the rope curtain, you will hear the talking voices of customers and Jazz in the background. With sake barrel decorated on the wall, this is a modern looking Japanese stand and drink bar.

This place is known for being cheap. It's a stand and drink bar widely used by the working people on their way home. Among them, couples and women groups stand out. This bar is women friendly with separate toilet for men and women and food is sold in prepaid tickets and the unused tickets are good for up 2 months so it's economical.

As a stand and drink bar, this place has an open feel like a spacious sports bar.

Comfort 1F
5 Chome 22-10
Toyotamakita
Nerima-ku, Tokyo-to

Open
11:00am-1:00am
Closed
Open throughout the year
Tel. 03-6915-8853

Direction
Get off at Seibu Ikebukuro line Nerima Station. walk 3-5 minutes

縄のれん・てんてん

練馬　　立ち飲み

　練馬の駅を降りて、ちょうど北側周辺に広がる盛り場の中にこの店はあります。縄暖簾をくぐって間口の広めの入り口から入れば、ＢＧＭのジャズと客の賑わいが耳に飛び込んできます。壁には酒樽が並べられて和風モダンな雰囲気。

　地元ではその安さと気安さから、サラリーマンが仕事帰りの止まり木に大いに利用している立ち飲み屋なのです。

　そんな中に若いカップルや女性同士のグループが目立ちますが、それはトイレが男女別であったりチケット販売機で購入する方式で、余ったチケットは次回も使える（２ヶ月間有効）といったことなど。女性に優しくて経済的だからかもしれません。それに見通しの広い店内は立ち飲み屋にしては広々としていてスポーツバーのような開放感があります。

東京都練馬区豊玉北5-22-10 コンフォート１階

営 午前11時から深夜1時まで
休 年中無休
TEL 03-6915-8853

アクセス
西武池袋線は練馬駅下車、徒歩３〜５分。

23 Izakaya ★ Hoshigumi

Sangenjaya **Wine Izakaya**

Speaking of Sangenjaya, it is famous for its Sankaku Area (Triangle Area) where the maze of restaurants and bars exist between the two main roads. Among them is an Izakaya called Hoshigumi. Located right in the middle of a back street, Sancha Sanban Gai. It has a red lantern written with the word "wine" in Katakana, hanging outside.

Once inside, you will come across an L-shaped counter. With wood furniture, this place is like a log house where you can feel the warmth and the coziness of the trees. It's not a big place, but you won't feel restricted or bored here.

Drinks include beer, highball, and cocktails but the main is the wine. With 10 kinds of red and white wine each, they also have 8 different kinds of carbonated alcohol drinks. Featuring both Japanese and Western dishes, everything looks delicious here.

---

2 Chome 13-10 Sangenjaya Setagaya-ku, Tokyo-to

Open
5:00pm-2:00am

Closed
Open throughout the year

Tel. 03-3487-9840

Direction
Exit at Sangenjaya Station using Tokyu Denentoshi Line. After entering Setagaya street opening, go to Tamagawa Street towards Futakotamagawa direction. After walking for a bit go into Sancha 3-bangai between ice cream shop and cafe. Destination located to the left. Look for a red lantern that says "wine".

いざかや★ほしぐみ

三軒茶屋　　**ワイン居酒屋**

　三軒茶屋といえば居酒屋が密集した交差点付近の三角州エリアが有名です。そんな中の「三茶3番街」の中にワインと書かれた赤提灯が目印です。

　中に入ると、目の前がL字のカウンター。木がふんだんに使われた店内でムキ出しの梁や柱に遠慮のいらない木肌のテーブルもあって、山小屋っぽいパブみたいな趣で居心地が良い。決して広くはないけど、窮屈さを感じさせないのは、やはり木の温もりがあるからです。

　お酒はビールやハイボール、サワーもあるけどメインはワイン。赤白各10種に泡モノが8種あるしメニューもそれに合わせた洋風から和風もありでどれもみな美味しい。

東京都世田谷区三軒茶屋2-13-10

営 夕方5時から深夜2時まで
休 年中無休
TEL 03-3487-9840

アクセス
東急田園都市線は三軒茶屋駅、世田谷通り口に出て、246(玉川通り)を二子玉川方面へしばらく行くとあるアイスクリーム屋とカフェの間の「三茶3番街」に入ってスグ左側、ワインと書かれた赤提灯が目印。

24 Zariganikichi

Nishi-Ogikubo **Yakitori**

"Yakitori" largely written on the indigo fabric curtain. Playing Rock music on the background, this is an eatery with an 8-seater L-shaped counter that effectively used the narrow space inside. The second floor is a group charter room which fits about 10 people. Not sure why, there is an old Nintendo Family Computer set there. Perhaps as a reminder of one's youth.

In a casual setting, customers come here to enjoy the conversation with the nice-looking chef. The name Zariganikichi comes from the base and secret hideout place from the childhood memories. It is the owner's intention that customers will never forget the innocence and playfulness when they were young.

Relax and have a glass of beer while watching the Yakitori being grilled.

3 Chome 40-12 Shōan Suginami-ku, Tokyo-to

Open
6:00pm-3:00am
Closed
Tuesday
Tel. 03-6750-8994

Direction
Turn right out of the JR Nishi-Ogikubo Station south exit. Located in front of you after passing through the alley that has Yakitori shop on both sides. 2-3 minutes walk

ザリガニ基地

西荻窪　　焼き鳥

　「ヤキトリ」と大きく書かれた藍色の暖簾が目立ちます。中に入るとＢＧＭにロックナンバーが流れています。

　小ぢんまりした店内は狭いスペースを有効利用した８人掛けのＬ字のカウンター。２階は10人くらい入れるお座敷になったグループ貸切用。どういうわけか昔のファミコンゲームもセットされています。

　狭い空間だけにホンワカムードの中、客はイケメン店長との会話を楽しみにやって来ます。店名の由来は、子供の頃遊んだ基地をイメージしていて、いつまでも童心を忘れずに飲んでもらいたいという意味からとか。焼き鳥はもちろん焼きたて、自分が注文した串が焼かれているのを眺めながらビールを一杯いただくのもなんだか落ち着けるのです。

東京都杉並区松庵3-40-12

営　夕方６時から深夜３時まで
休　火曜日
TEL　03-6750-8994

アクセス
ＪＲ西荻窪駅南口を出て右へ。焼鳥屋さんが左右に並ぶ路地を抜けてスグ目の前。徒歩２〜３分。

25 Sumibi Yakitori Binchō

Nogata | **Yakitori**

Rope curtains are the landmark. Located in a shopping street a little away from the station. A typical Yakitori eatery. Inside, shiny black wooden beams like the old country style house can be seen. Very calm atmosphere. If you look at the left, there is an L-shaped counter that seats 9, built around the grill area. And on the right-hand side are tables with divides which provide some privacy. This place can accommodate 30 people total.

Loved by the local people. This restaurant caters domestic high quality chicken from Tottori prefecture. Menu is not limited to yakitori. Italian, Mexican and other western style foods are served here. It's best to go with a group so you can try out many different dishes. Mostly office workers, surprisingly, some women customers also go by themself. On the weekends and holidays, it's filled with family crowd.

---

6 Chome 29-9
Nogata Nakano-ku,
Tokyo-to

Open
5:00pm-2:00am
Closed
Open throughout the year
Tel. 03-3338-1007

Direction
Turn right at Seibu Shinjuku Line Nogata ticket gate. Go towards Shin-Ome direction after entering Kitahara shopping district. Located next to electronic shop after walking for about 100 meters.

炭火やきとり備長(びんちょう)

| 野方 | 焼き鳥 |

縄暖簾が目印の同店は、駅からちょっと離れた商店街の中にあります。いかにも焼き鳥屋さんっぽくて、中に入ると古民家風の梁が黒光りして、落ち着いてゆっくり出来る雰囲気です。左を見ると、焼き場を囲むようにL字のカウンター9席。そして右側には仕切りのあるテーブルが並んでいて、全部で30人は入れそうです。

鳥取の大山地鶏と国産朝びきを扱う店として地元の人にも愛されています。メニューは焼き鳥だけに留まらず、各種和風からトマト鍋やメキシコ風など洋風の鍋まで頂けるからグループ客にはお勧めです。客はもっぱら帰宅前にちょいと一杯というサラリーマンですが、女性の独り客も意外に多くて週末や休日は家族連れで賑わいます。

東京都中野区野方6-29-9

営 夕方5時から深夜2時まで
休 年中無休
TEL 03-3338-1007

アクセス
西武新宿線野方改札を出て右側に。北原商店街に入って新青梅方面に100メートルほど歩いた家電屋さんの隣り。

26 Hamauo

Nishi-Ogikubo **Kaisen Izakaya**

The area surrounding JR Nishi-Ogikubo Station has long been a battlefield for Izakaya restaurants. Recently, many unique Izayaka are opening here which has been getting some attention. Meanwhile, Hamauo is one of those Izakaya specializing in fish.

Stylish interior with a small counter and tables. You can enjoy sashimi and sake quietly. A place with Japanese accent which makes you forget the busy street outside. Reasonably priced. Try many kinds of sashimi and Japanese food in small portion. Sit at the counter to watch the young Master Chef cut fish and enjoy small talk with him. You will likely return to this Izakaya from time to time. It's relatively less busy with fewer customers when they first open in the evening. So if you want to take your time to eat and relax that would be the best time to go.

Ozawa building 1F
3 Chome 25-7
Nishiogiminami
Suginami-ku,
Tokyo-to

Open
6:00pm-1:00am
Closed
Sunday
Tel. 03-3247-2477

Direction
Exit at JR Chuo Line Nishi-Ogikubo Station south exit. Immediately to the right after walking along the right lane. 1 minute walk

浜魚

`西荻窪` `海鮮居酒屋`

　ＪＲ西荻窪駅周辺は昔から多くの居酒屋が営業している激戦区ですが、ここ最近になって新しい個性的な居酒屋がオープンしていて注目を集めています。そんな中、魚にこだわった和食のお店がここ。

　小さなカウンターに小さなテーブルが並ぶスタイリッシュな店内でお刺身をつまみながら静かに日本酒を頂けば、外の喧噪も忘れて和風の異空間へトリップできます。お値段もリーズナブルでお刺身も少しずつ色んな種類を頂けるからプチ和食体験をするのには打って付けの店です。カウンター越しに見る包丁さばきを見ながら、その若い主人と色んな会話を楽しめばこの店がいつしか自分にとって居酒屋を超えた隠れ家となっていることでしょう。特に夕方のオープン時間は比較的客が少ないのでゆっくりと過ごせるからオススメなのです。

東京都杉並区西荻南
3-25-7　小沢ビル１Ｆ

営　夕方６時から１３時
休　日曜日
℡　03-3247-2477

アクセス
ＪＲ中央線西荻窪駅南口を下りて線路沿い右へ行ってすぐ右側。徒歩１分。

27 Bakatare Zutchan

Nakano **Yakiton**

With clips of European newspaper articles covering soccer posted on the wall, Bakatare is more like an open café than a yakiton eatery. A counter that sits 7 and three small round tables. With the wood deck, you can sit outside and enjoy the delicious cold beer in cool breeze during the summer days.

The origin of the name Bakatare means insanely tasty sauce. Carefully prepared. Tender and no distinct smell. Their skewers are delicious and beyond expectation.

More than a typical yakiton eatery, the menu here includes *Kochori* (a kim chee flavored salad) found in the Yakiniku restaurant. It is the perfect place to enjoy the deliciousness of yakiton.

5 Chome 36-3 Nakano Nakano-ku, Tokyo-to

Open
5:00pm-12:00am
Closed
Sunday, Monday, and Holidays
Tel. 03-3389-2229

Direction
Exit at JR Nakano Station north exit. Turn right before the "aka chō-chin" tavern parallels to Sun Mall at Fureai Road. Located between the sequence of convenience stores.

ばかたれ ずっちゃん

`中野` `焼きトン`

　店内の壁にサッカーの記事が載ったヨーロッパの新聞が貼られていたりして、焼きトン屋さんというよりは何やら開放的なカフェといった風情の同店。カウンターが7席にテーブルが3個。更に店先はオープンデッキになっていて、暑い夏場は気持いい風に吹かれながら冷えたビールが美味しそうです。

　店名の由来は、バカ美味しいタレという意味。確かに頂けるモツ焼きは丁寧な仕事振りで繊細な食感に柔らかさといい臭さみの無さといい、これはもはやモツ焼きを超えた立派な肉料理といえるほど。

　またメニューにはモツ焼屋さんには珍しい、焼き肉のメニューにあるチョレギサラダもある。モツ肉の旨さを堪能するのは打って付けな一軒であります。

東京都中野区中野5-36-3

- 営 夕方5時から12時まで
- 休 日曜と月曜が祝日の日
- TEL 03-3389-2229

【アクセス】
JR中野駅は北口に出て、サンモールに並行する「ふれあいロード」の居酒屋「赤ちょうちん」の手前を右に入ってコンビニの並び。

28 Shokudō Osaka

Sangenjaya **Izakaya Shokudō**

2 Chome 13-9
Sangenjaya
Setagaya-ku,
Tokyo-to

Open
10:00pm-11:00am
Closed
No scheduled holidays
Tel. 03-3419-4129

Direction
Take the Denentoshi Tokyu line and get off at Sangenjaya Station. Exit at Sancha Patio exit and take the left 246 national highway Route towards Komaba direction. Turn right at the corner of Italian tomatoes. Located to the right after walking for a while. 3-4 minutes walk

Speaking of the night life in Sangenjaya, everyone knows the sankakusu (the triangle area). A place where smell of Showa remain intact. Numerous pubs and eateries are jammed inside in the triangle area. Business stays open till the morning hours.

At the corner of such busy street, a red noren curtain caught our eyes. It was past 12 midnight, but this place was still open.

"Irasshaimase" a cheerful woman chef will greet you when you enter. Shokudo Osaka is an all-nighter cafeteria catering to people who finish their work late at night. Some come for breakfast before heading to work. Customers include taxi drivers, nurses, office workers and men who stay up all night drinking.

The woman chef's carefree and bright personality, makes even the first time customer feel at home.

Their specialty is the dried fish and clear soup that uses only bonito directly from Izu. If you want to taste Japanese dried fish, we recommend you come here and try it out.

食堂おさか

三軒茶屋　　**居酒屋食堂**

　三軒茶屋の盛り場といえば、昭和の香りそのまま残る通称三角州という飲食店の密集地帯が有名。

　そんな中の路地の一角に、紅色の暖簾が目に入る。手元の時計を見ればもぉ夜の12時を廻っているがまだ営業中です。

　「いらっしゃいませぇ！」と元気な女将さんの声で迎えてくれます。まさにここは深夜食堂。お客さんは夜勤明けのタクシードライバーやら、看護師さん。朝は通勤前の朝食を食べるＯＬさん、それに夜通し飲んでるサラリーマンもいたりする。

　屈託の無い明るい性格の女将さんだから、初めての客もスグに常連さん気分になれる。

　ここの自慢は干物や澄し汁に使うカツオ節も全て伊豆直送ということ。日本の干物を味わいたいならお勧めなのです。

東京都世田谷区三軒茶屋2-13-9

営 夜10時から翌朝11時まで
休 不定休
TEL 03-3419-4129

アクセス
東急田園都市線、三軒茶屋駅は三茶パティオ口に出て左国道246号線を駒場方面へ進み、イタリアントマトの角を右に曲がってしばらく行った右側。徒歩3〜4分。

29 Sasurai

Sangenjaya **Chuhai Izakaya**

2F 2 Chome 10-12 Sangenjaya Setagaya-ku, Tokyo-to

Open
8:00pm-2:00am
Closed
No scheduled holidays
Tel. 03-3418-6323

Direction
Take the Denentoshi Tokyu line and get off at Sangenjaya Station. Take the national highway 246 towards Komazawa direction. Turn right before passing Tokyo-Mitsubishi UFJ Bank. Located on the second floor to the left after walking for 3-4 minutes.

Without putting out a sign, this place is on the second floor with an entrance that is hard to find. Once upstairs, customers are greeted by the manager with a warm "irasshaimase".

It has counters and table seats with a capacity of 15 people. Looking up the beams, the ceiling is wide with a natural feel that creates an open and cozy atmosphere. A completely different dimension that makes the hustle and bustle atmosphere moments ago seems unreal.

This Izakaya is famous among the locals as a place where many kinds of shochu cocktail drinks are served.

Mixed drinks that are common in downtown Tokyo. Cocktail drinks using the award winning Kinmiya shochu as the base and adding fruit juice or other flavored carbonated beverages manufactured by the Tokyo Inryo company can be tasted here.

Delicious and unique fusion cuisine compromises the East and West! If you haven't experienced the new fusion style Japanese food, this is a place for you.

さすらい

三軒茶屋　**酎ハイ居酒屋**

　看板も出て無くて、実にわかりにくい入口から階段を上がってお２階へ行くと、「いらっしゃいませ！」と店長に迎えられます。

　店内はカウンターとテーブル席が並びキャパは15人程。見上げると梁があったりして、ナチュラルな落ち着いた空間が広がり、先ほどの街の喧噪が嘘のようで、まさに異空間。

　このお店は様々な焼酎のカクテル（酎ハイ）が頂けるお店として地元では有名なスポットなのです。

　東京は下町ではお馴染みの、割モノメーカーであるトーイン（東京飲料）から出てる色んな割モノ飲料と金宮の焼酎でつくるここの酎ハイの味は様々な味があって面白い。

　ちなみに料理も和洋折衷系でユニークで美味しい！未だ体験したことのない人は新しい和食の世界を堪能できますよ。

東京都世田谷区三軒茶屋2-10-12　２階

営　夜８時から深夜２時
休　不定休
TEL　03-3418-6323

[アクセス]
田園都市線の三軒茶屋駅を出て国道246を駒沢方面へ。右側にある東京三菱ＵＦＪ銀行の手前を右へ。３〜４分歩いた左側の２階（看板ナシ）。

30 Taishū kappō Ajitome

Sangenjaya **Izakaya**

With a 47 year history, this place has long been a favorite of the locals and actors from the theaters and playhouse nearby. It is well known as a place where entertainers and intellectuals come and drink from the morning.

The place may seem cluttered and messy at first. However, it is calm and laid-back. You can drink and even fall asleep here.

The lady Master is famous here and she always greets everyone with enthusiasm and smile. The wall inside is occupied with pictures, posters and menu written in different paper sizes and colors. A unique and well-established Izakaya where you can enjoy authentic Japanese dishes such as puffer, eel, whale, goosefish at a relatively affordable price.

---

4 Chome 23-7 Taishido Setagaya-ku, Tokyo-to

Open
9:30am-12:00am (24:00)Saturday, Sunday and holidays 3:00pm-12:00am

Closed
Twice a month on Mondays

Tel. 03-3412-9973

Direction
Find the police box at the Sangenjaya Station of the Denentoshi Line. Enter the Suzuran Street located next to the police box. Destination to the right side of Suzuran Street.

大衆割烹・味とめ

| 三軒茶屋 | 居酒屋 |

　この店は知る人ぞ知る何と創業47年の老舗の居酒屋さんです。古くからの常連さんも来るし、近くの劇場で芝居のはねた劇団の役者さんたちがよく打ち上げに利用したり、芸能人や文化人らがお馴染みにする朝から飲める名物居酒屋です。

店構えからして雑然としてるけど、中に入ればもっと雑然としていて、超ドメスティックでオールドだから気兼ねなく飲みながら寝っ転がっても平気なところです。ようするに凄くリラックス出来るというわけです。

そんな店の名物マダムはいつも笑顔で出迎えてくれます。しかし、店内壁中にメニューの短冊が張りめぐらされていて、フグもあれば、鯨に鰻、あんこうもなど、本格和食を比較的安く堪能できる名店なのです。

東京都世田谷太子堂4-23-7

営 朝9時30分から深夜12時（お客しだい）土日祝は午後3時から12時
休 毎月2回、不定期の月曜日
Tel 03-3412-9973

アクセス
田園都市線は三軒茶屋駅を出て、交番の横のすずらん通りを入りしばらくいった奥の右側。

31 Ichifuji

Nakano **Yankton**

Located in Nakano station where redevelopment has rapidly progressed. An area where changes have taken place dramatically as a result of high-rise mansions and office buildings construction boom.

Found in the basement of the food alley in the north exit from the station. This place was established on the day when the Second World War ended in 1945. It started as a moveable food stall. Soon after, it was moved to a location near the south exit of the station. Due to the redevelopment, it got relocated again to the current location twenty some years ago. It's considered the number one or number two longest established Izakaya in the Nakano area.

There is an L shaped counter and two tables with a capacity of 16. This place is filled with the nostalgic mood of Showa.

Using the same blackboards that have been used for generations and the menus were written in unique terminology such as tonmotsu for yakiton and hontoriniku for yakitori.

Noi building underground first floor 2 Chome 25-6 Nakano Nakano-ku, Tokyo-to

Open
6:00pm-11:30pm
Closed
Sunday and Holidays
Tel. 03-3381-9102

Direction
Exit at JR Nakano south exit with the rotary road. Located underground of the building to the left where there is a gym.

いちふじ

中野　　焼きトン

　最近は再開発が進んで、高層マンションやオフィスビルの建設ラッシュですっかり様変わりしている中野駅周辺にこの店はあります。

　北口駅前のビルの地下にある飲食街。創業なんと昭和20年終戦の日。元々屋台からだけど、スグにこの南口にお店を構え、やがて再開発でこのビルに入ったのが20数年前というから中野でも1～2位を争う老舗の居酒屋なのです。

　店内はL字のカウンターとテーブルが2つ程。16人くらいは入れるキャパ。なんとも昭和のノスタルジックなムードが漂っている。

　先代の頃から使用しているメニューの看板に、やきとんを「とんもつ」、焼き鳥を「本鶏肉」と、なんとも味のある字で書いています。

東京都中野区中野2-25-6
ノイビル地下1階

営 夕方6時から夜11時30分まで
休 日曜日・祝日
TEL 03-3381-9102

アクセス
JR中野区南口のロータリー駅を背にして左側にあるジムの入るビルの地下。

South Area

南部地区

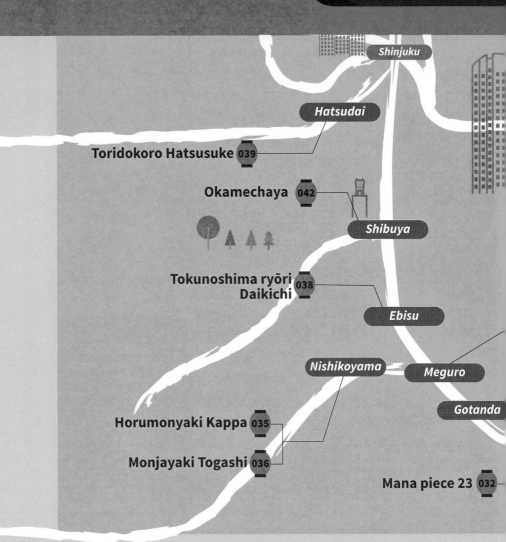

Shibuya-ku（渋谷区）
Minato-ku（港区）
Meguro-ku（目黒区）
Shinagawa-ku（品川区）
Ōta-ku（太田区）

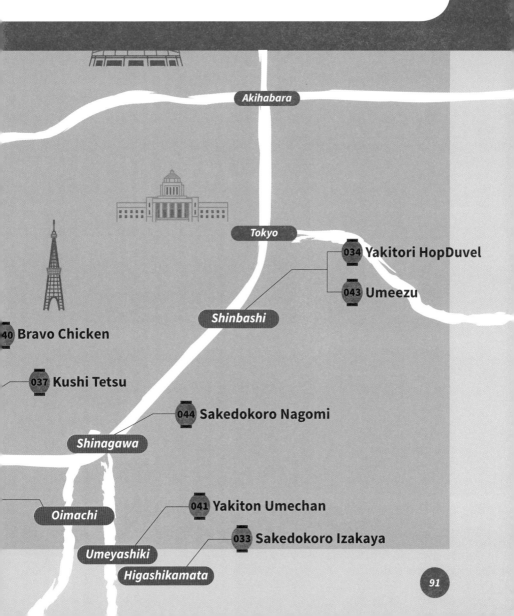

Mana piece 23

Oimachi | **Yakiton**

Decorated with a pink store sign, no one would perceive this place as a Yakiton eatery by its appearance. Moreover, the name of the store is very mysterious but we will leave that for you to find out directly from the store.

Because the owner was originally a Chinese food chef, this place features not only yakiton, it also offers Chinese food such as fried rice and other popular dishes.

In addition, different from other yakiton places where meats are pre-seasoned, at this place, customers sprinkle salt on the meat by themselves. It is said that this salt brings out the best flavor of the meat because it is a natural sea salt from Amami region.

This is a small venue with a counter that sits only 7. Therefore it is not a place to visit with a big group but rather a place for one person or a group of two or three people.

---

4 Chome 12-24 Ōi Shinagawa-ku, Tokyo-to

Open
5:00pm-12:00am
Closed
Tuesday
Tel. 03-6303-8689

Direction
Exit at Oimachi Station Chuonishi direction exit. Walk straight and go under Ōi Riku Bridge. After passing the bridge, turn right at Crystal building and walk for a while. 7-8 minutes walk

まなpiece23

　大井町　　　焼きトン

　店構えからして誰もやきとん屋さんとは思わないピンクをあしらった看板が目印です。またこの奇妙な店名も気になるが、それは店にいって直接聞いてもらいたいです。

　ここの特徴は串焼きのやきとんの他に御主人が元中華のコックだったため珍しくチャーハンといったしっかりとご飯ものの中華料理のメニューも頂けます。

　そしてやきとんの食べ方はちょっと他のやきとん屋さんとは違い味を付けずに焼いた肉に自分で塩を付けて食べるというなんとも野趣溢れる方法。ちなみにその塩は奄美地方の塩を使っているから甘いうま味が肉の味を引き立ててくれます。

　カウンター7人といった小さなスポットだから、大勢でいくのではなく、訪れるなら1人か2人〜3人で行くことをお勧めします。

東京都品川区大井4-12-24

営 午後5時〜24時
休 火曜日
TEL 03-6303-8689

[アクセス]
大井町駅中央西方面口に降りて真っ直ぐ大井陸橋をくぐってクリスタルビルを右へ曲がってしばらくいったところ。徒歩7〜8分。

33 Sakedokoro Izakaya

Higashikamata **Izakaya**

1 Chome 12-8 Higashikamata Ōta-ku, Tokyo-to

Open
Lunchtime 11:00am-2:00pm Dinner 6:00pm-3:00am
Closed
Tuesday
Tel. 03-6424-8837

Direction
After exiting from Keikyū-sen Umeyashiki Station, cross the first Keihin Umeyashiki Station entrance intersection. Enter the Umeyashiki East Shopping Street and turn right at FamilyMart. Located to the right after walking for about 100 meters of Azumadōri shinboku-kai Shopping Street. 8 minutes walk

This diner's name is really unique. It's simply called Izakaya—a generic name for a place to eat and drink. Easy to understand indeed. The location is within the residential area, away from the station where tourists are unlikely to visit. A great place to get a feel of ordinary Japanese downtown life.

This place used to be a sushi venue. The new owner took over but everything was kept as is. No wondered it has the glass case where sushi/sashimi were kept and displayed. Surprisingly, the chef is very young. A 22 years old fellow. Apparently the owner scouted him from a big Izakaya chain store where he used to work.

With a capacity of 14-15 people. Customers are local couples and workers on their way home. During late hours, people working at other restaurants/eateries also stop by.

In fact, you can drink and have a meal here at a very low price. During the day, single elderly come here to meet other elderlies. This place is like a kitchen where people get together and chat.

酒処・居酒屋

| 東蒲田 | 居酒屋 |

　このお店の店名が実にユニークです。なんと「居酒屋」。実に解りやすい。場所は駅から住宅地の中に入り込んだところで、まず観光客が来るところではありません。でも日本の下町のなんとも落ち着いた生活を感じるにはうってつけなのです。

　元々この店舗はお寿司屋さんだったそうで、そのまま居抜きで営業しているとのこと。道理でショウケースといいお寿司やさんの面影が残っている。それにしても店長さんが若い！　何と弱冠22歳。実はオーナーに請われて、以前勤めていた大きな居酒屋さんからスカウトされたんだとか。

　キャパは14～15人ってところかな。客スジは地元の夫婦連れや、仕事帰りの工具さんも。夜も遅くなれば同業関係の方も仕事上がりに立ち寄っていくといいます。

　実際、飯も食えるし、安く飲める。早い時間も独り暮らしのお年寄りの集会所というか、台所みたいになっているみたいです。

東京都大田区東蒲田1-12-8

営　午前11時から午後2時はランチタイム。夕方6時から翌3時まで営業
休　火曜日
TEL　03-6424-8837

アクセス
京急線梅屋敷駅を出て第1京浜梅屋敷駅入口交差点を渡り、梅屋敷東通り商店街へ入ってファミマを右へ。東通り親睦会商店街に入って100㍍程行った右側、徒歩8分。

34 Yakitori HopDuvel

Shinbashi **Yakitori**

A little distance from the hustle and fast-paced Shinbashi station is a long-established Japanese Yakitori shop. A bit hard to find but look for a picture of a big rooster painted on the exterior wall. When you open the wooden door and enter this place, you will see a counter bar with stools. This is a counter only restaurant. Behind the bar, Yakitori are grilled over charcoal.

HopDuvel is a place where East meets West. Drinking Belgium beer, while eating yakitori.

People come here to taste the authentic Belgian beers and upscale yakitori made to order. A rich experience found only here. For your information, sake, shochu are also available other than beers.

**Komakura building 1F 3 Chome
3-4 Minato-ku,
Shinbashi, Tokyo-to**

Open
Monday-Friday
6:00pm-11:00pm
Saturday
5:00pm-10:00pm
Closed
Sunday & holidays
Tel. 03-3581-7773

Direction
Exit at JR Shinbashi Station Karasumoriguchi exit. Looking at New Shimbashi building on the right-hand side, go toward Hibiya Street. After passing Shinbashi 3 Chome police box, turn left at the second street. It will be located at the right corner past the first crossroad.

焼き鳥ホップデュベル

新橋　　焼き鳥

　新橋駅の盛り場の喧噪からちょいと離れたこのあたりは、ポツリとある和食系の老舗を見かけたりする渋い場所ですが、目印は壁に大きなニワトリの絵です。さほど広くない木製ドアを開けて中に入ると、意外やカウンターだけの店でバー？　かと思えばカウンターの中では熾した炭に焼き鳥が焼かれており不思議な感じの焼き鳥屋さんなのです。
　聞けばベルギービールと焼き鳥という和洋折衷のこだわりのお店です。

　日本では珍しいヨーロッパでも個性的な味で有名な本格的なベルギーの地ビールと高級な焼き鳥が頂けます。本物にこだわったちょっとリッチな焼き鳥体験が楽しめるのでした。ちなみにビール以外に日本酒や焼酎も用意されています。

東京都港区新橋
3-3-4　駒倉ビル1階

営　夕方6時から11時（月～金）。土曜は5時から10時まで。
休　日曜日・祝日
TEL　03-3581-7773

アクセス
JR新橋駅は烏森口を出て、ニュー新橋ビルを右側に見ながら真っ直ぐ日比谷通りを目指して、新橋三丁目交番前を過ぎて2筋目を左へ。最初の十字路を過ぎてスグ右角。

35 Horumonyaki Kappa

Nishikoyama   **Horumonyaki Izakaya**

The shopping streets around here remain a nostalgic charm of downtown taste. Horumonyaki Kappa offers a friendly atmosphere. Yellow sign says Horumonyaki and the nawanoren, rope curtains and a bus stop sign can be found in the storefront.

The interior is simple, decorated in clean white-wood tone. The dim track light provides calmness. Silver duct vents are installed above the counter which accommodates 10 people. Additional space available on the second floor for 10 people as well.

This Tokyo location is said to be a branch of a long established Horumonyaki restaurant founded in Yamagata. The first restaurant was opened more than 55 years ago. This Tokyo location uses the exact same secret sauce and ingredients such as pork, rice, miso, and even the traditional charcoal grills (shichirin) as the original restaurant.

---

6 Chome
2-3 Koyama
Shinagawa-ku,
Tokyo-to

Open
6:00pm-2:00am
Closed
Monday
Tel. 03-3787-8854

Direction
Get off at Nishikoyama Station using Tokyu Meguro Line. Enter right into the shopping street that is on the rotary side. Located on the right-hand side, immediately after turning right.

ホルモン焼　かっぱ

西小山　　**ホルモン焼き居酒屋**

　このあたり商店街は下町風情の残る肩のこらない所。この店もそんなフランクなムードなところです。縄暖簾にホルモンの黄色い看板が目印。店先にはバス停の看板も置いてあって遊び心が面白いのです。

　店内は白木を基調とした清潔感ある内装で、ダウンライトが程良い薄暗さで落ち着きます。各カウンターの上からは銀色のダクトが並んで、さっと10人は座れそうです。でもってお2階はお座敷になってて、そこも10人は座れます。

　同店は山形で創業55年にもなる有名老舗ホルモン焼き屋の東京支店としてオープンした店で、ここで使われている秘伝のタレを始め、豚肉も米も炭も味噌も、七輪まで山形の本店と同じモノを使用しています。

東京都品川区小山6-2-3

営 夕方6時から深夜2時まで
休 月曜日
TEL 03-3787-8854

アクセス
東急目黒線は西小山駅を出てロータリー脇にある、左右2つある商店街の入口を右に入ってすぐ右側。

36 Monjayaki Togashi

Nishikoyama **Monjayaki Izakaya**

Monjayaki is a type of Japanese pan-fried batter pancake with various ingredients such as seafood, meat and vegetables. Monjayaki Togashi is located at Nishikoyama, a town with lively shopping streets and a short distance from Meguro. A big spatula object stands out at the doorstep. A typical look of a downtown storefront. Once inside, Teppanyaki grill is built-in at each table. A spacious Japanese style room fits roughly 30 people. You don't need to travel to Tsukishima, a popular tourist destination, to taste authentic Monjayaki. At this place, you can find real delicious Monjayaki and feel welcomed. In the late hours, local dads or young men and women come here to hang out. On the weekends, families gather at this restaurant. A great spot to observe lively Japanese family life.

6 Chome
2-5 Koyama
Shinagawa-ku,
Tokyo-to

Open
12:00pm-2:00am
Closed
No scheduled holidays
Tel. 03-6426-6338

Direction
Exit at Nishikoyama Station using Tokyu Meguro Line. Find the side of the traffic rotary where the entrance is a Taiyaki and Yakiton restaurant. Enter the shopping district and it will be located at the immediate right.

もんじゃ焼　とがし

`西小山`　`もんじゃ焼き居酒屋`

　目黒からほど近い街で活気のある商店街のある西小山。そんな商店街の中で営業しているもんじゃ焼屋さんです。玄関口には大きなコテのオブジェが目立っています。いかにも下町っぽい店構えです。

　中に入ると、堀り炬燵の小上がりに鉄板のテーブルが並びます。ゆったりした日本のお座敷スタイルで、ざっと30人は入れそうです。

　観光地と化したいまの月島にわざわざ行かなくても、本格的なもんじゃが頂けると地元のもんじゃ好きには温かく迎えられています。

　遅い時間は地元のお父さんやお兄ちゃんにお姉さん。土日になれば家族連れで賑わう日本人の日常を覗けるお店です。

東京都品川区小山6-2-5

営 お昼12時から深夜2時まで
休 不定休
TEL 03-6426-6338

アクセス
東急目黒線は西小山駅を出て、目の前のロータリー脇にある、入口がたい焼きさんと焼きトン屋さんの商店街を入ってスグ右側。

37 Kushi Tetsu

Gotanda **Teppanyaki Izakaya**

Out from the back streets that extends from the east exit of Gotanda, Kushi Tetsu lies in the high-rise condo county near Osaki area.

With intimate lighting and the background Jazz music, this place has a relaxed atmosphere. One table and an open kitchen counter which accommodate up to 15 people. Behind the counter is a large teppan hot plate where food is prepared right before your eyes.

While food tastes great simply by steaming on the hot iron plate, it also makes the meat soft and tender. This is a wonderful way to cook food. It brings out the best flavor of any kind of ingredients. Dipped with your choice of yuzu pepper, citrus dressing or sea salt.

By the way, this restaurant uses olive oil which has less smell and makes the food tastes better than the regular cooking oil.

Iijima new building 1F 2 Chome 7-10 Shinagawa-ku, Higashigotanda, Tokyo-to

Open
5:00pm-2:00am
Closed
Wednesday
Tel. 03-3443-5801

Direction
Turn right at JR Gotanda Station east exit. Turn left at the first corner after entering the road between Tokyu store and glasses shop. Next, turn right at the corner of fresh fish tavern. Make an immediate left after turning right at the corner.

串テツ

`五反田`　`鉄板焼き居酒屋`

　五反田といえば東口正面に広がる有楽街からは外れて、やや大崎方面の高層マンション群の中にポツンとあるのが同店。

　落ち着いた雰囲気の照明にＢＧＭはジャズが流れています。手前にはテーブルと10数人は座れそうなカウンター席。そのカウンターの前には大きな鉄板があって、目の前で焼いてくれるという趣向です。

　鉄板で蒸し焼きにするだけのシンプルな調理法ながら、肉など柔らかく仕上がってどれもこれも素材の旨さが充分に引き出されていて美味しく頂けます。それらをゆず胡椒かポン酢や岩塩に付けてお好みで頂けます。

　ちなみに鉄板に引く油は、匂いが少なく素材のうま味を引き出すオリーブオイルを使用しています。

東京都品川区東五反田2-7-10　飯島ニュービルディング1階

営 夕方5時から深夜2時まで
休 水曜日
TEL 03-3443-5801

アクセス
ＪＲ五反田駅は東口を出て右へ。東急ストアーとメガネ屋さんの間を入り、最初の角を左へ。次に鮮魚居酒屋の角を右に曲がってスグ左へ入った左側。

38 Tokunoshima ryōri Daikichi

Ebisu **Tokunoshima Cuisine Izakaya**

In the area near the west exit of Ebisu station, you will find various new and old established Izayaka mixing together. Among them is a cozy and nostalgic restaurant specializes Tokunoshima cuisine. Tables and open tatami space accommodate 50 people. Daikichi is one of the oldest Izayaka in the vicinity with a 35 year history, dating back to the Showa period.

Surrounded by bottles of specialty brown sugar Shochu made in Tokunoshima will definitely catch your attention. Authentic Southern Japan and Okinawa food can be tasted here.

If you are lucky, you might be able to hear the Island folksongs sung by the owner accompanied by the Sanshin—a three strings music instrument. Thanks to the owner, this place is open and friendly.

1 Chome 7-11 Ebisunishi Shibuya-ku, Tokyo-to

Open
5:00pm-12:00am
Closed
Sunday & Holidays
Tel. 03-3496-8904

Direction
Exit at JR Ebisu Station west exit and go toward the right direction with the public toilets. Turn left after crossing the signal and go right at the first corner. It will be located to the right after walking for a while. Look for a yellow signboard.

徳之島料理・大吉

恵比寿　　**徳之島料理居酒屋**

　恵比寿の西口側は新旧の居酒屋さんが入り乱れてズラッと並んでいます。そんな中でも、ノスタルジックな雰囲気を醸し出している同店は徳之島料理の居酒屋さんです。店内は手前と奥にテーブルが有り奥にはお座敷もある。広々として、全部で50人は入れる大箱でまさに昭和の居酒屋さん。ここ恵比寿で何と35年というこの界隈では一番古い老舗です。

　ふと目に止まるのはズラッと並ぶ徳之島の黒糖焼酎のボトル。本格的な島料理を肴に南国気分を味わえます。

　興がのればご店主が三線（さんしん）を取り出して島の民謡を一節唸ったりすることもあるとか。なんとも開放的でフレンドリーな雰囲気はこの店の御主人のおかげなのかもしれません。

東京都渋谷区恵比寿西1-7-11

営 夕方5時から12時まで
休 日曜日・祝日
TEL 03-3496-8904

アクセス
JR恵比寿駅西口を出て、公衆トイレのある右方向へ。信号を渡って左折して、1つ目の角を右へ入りしばらく行った右。黄色い看板が目印。

39 Toridokoro Hatsusuke

Hatsudai **Yakitori**

Speaking of Hatusdai, it is the nearest station to the New National Theater Tokyo. Located right by the theater, Toridokoro Hatsusuke is a rare restaurant that is a ramen shop and a Yakitori shop. Two separate entrance. If you want ramen only, go to the left, and you will be seated at the counter. By the way, you can order ramen after eating Yakitori.

This is a business district so majority of their customers are office workers. Among them, about 30% are women, which is a pretty high percentage. Many kinds of yakitori are cooked in different seasonings. With various side menus, you can almost call this place a Yakitori Bar.

Enomoto building 1F 1 Chome 2-2 Honmachi Shibuya-ku, Tokyo-to

Open
5:30pm-2:00am
Closed
Open throughout the year
Tel. 03-6276-1163

Direction
Immediately located in front of you after taking Keio New Line Hatsudai Station Central Exit (north entrance).

とり処・初介

`初台` `焼き鳥`

　初台といえば新国立劇場の最寄り駅。その劇場の真横にあるのが同店。鳥白湯スープのラーメン屋さんも一緒に営業する珍しい焼き鳥の店です。入口は別々だが店内に入るとつながっていて、ラーメンだけを食べたい人は左の「濃厚鶏そば・麺屋武一」の入口から入ってカウンター席で頂けます。因みに焼き鳥を頂いた後の〆のラーメンは注文できます。

　周辺がオフィス街のため客の大半がサラリーマンでその内3割ぐらいは女子というから女子率高めのお店です。焼き鳥メニューは種類も豊富だし、色んな味付けがされてて、サイドメニューも充実していて焼き鳥バルといってもいいかもしれません。

東京都渋谷区本町
1-2-2　榎本ビル1階

営 夕方5時30分から
　翌深夜2時まで
休 年中無休
TEL 03-6276-1163

アクセス
京王新鮮初台駅中央口（北口）を出てスグ目の前。

40 Bravo Chicken

Meguro **Stand and Drink Bar**

A rare fried chicken to-go place and a standing bar. To find this place, look for the fast-food looking sign. Once inside, there is an L shaped counter which fits roughly 10 people.

Here, Japanese style fried chicken Karaage is their specialty. Chicken is fried after the order is placed. Karaage can be a beer appetizer or a main dish at a meal. It's also a popular item for bento lunch boxes. Many elderly locals who live alone order them as take out. Housewives in the neighborhood also come here and buy them to take home.

People travel long distance to get a taste of it after hearing how good it is. Women especially. If you like Japanese style fried chicken, this is a place you don't want to miss.

---

3 Chome 1-2 Meguro Meguro-ku, Tokyo-to

Open
Takeout from 11:30am-2:00pm & 4:30pm -10:00pm
Standing drink 5:00pm-11:00pm

Closed
Tuesday

Tel. 070-6484-2080

Direction
Take the Yamate Street from Tokyu Toyoko Line Naka-Meguro Station. Located near Dendo intersection. 12-13 minutes walk

ブラボーチキン

目黒　　立ち飲み

　唐揚げで飲ませるめずらしい立ち飲み屋です。一見するとファストフードのような看板が目印です。中に入るとくの字のカウンター。斜め45度に陣取れば10人は入れそうです。

　ここは注文をしてから目の前で揚げたてを頂けるシステムで、これを肴に飲むビールが実に美味しい。ちなみにお持ち帰りもやっていて地元の独り暮らしの中高年が家呑みをするためや、ご近所の主婦がご飯のおかずにと買って帰っていきます。また遠方から噂を聞き付けてやってくる客もいたりするという。それも女性客が多いとか。唐揚げ好きならオススメです。

東京都目黒区目黒3-1-2

営 テイクアウト11時30分から14時　16時30分から22時　立ち飲み17時から23時まで
休 火曜日定休日
TEL 070-6484-2080

アクセス
東急東横線中目黒駅から山手通りを歩いて田道交差点近く徒歩12〜13分。

41 Yakiton Umechan

Umeyashiki   **Yakiton**

Walking straight along the long stretch of shopping street, there is a restaurant called Umechan. Look for the sign that says "Yakiton", and a red noren curtain. Glass door allows you to see all the way back, a place with openness. Once inside, you will notice this place is bigger than it appears to be from outside. Accommodates 20 people. There are tables and counter seats to choose from.

The chef is a young woman, which is rare in this kind of restaurant. She is referred as Kayo chan by the customers who come here often. Kayo chan cooks and prepare each skewer carefully. 4th year in business so it is still new. It is called Umechan because it's close to Umeyashiki Station. The recommended dishes are the miso yakiton and motsu stew.

kawabata building 1F 1 Chome 3-4 Ōta-ku, Kamata, Tokyo-to

Open
5:00pm-12:00am
Closed
Wednesday
Tel. 03-6424-8420

Direction
Get off at Keihin Express Railway Station Umeyashiki. Not to cross the railroad crossing, walk Puramoru Umeyashiki shopping street for 200 meters. Past the main street and enter the road between family restaurant and dry cleaning. Walk for a little bit and look for a red shop curtain on the left side.

やきとん 梅ちゃん

梅屋敷　　**焼きトン**

　長い長〜い商店街をしばらく行くとこの店はあります。やきとんと書かれた赤い暖簾が目印です。ガラス戸だから店内奥まで見渡せて、開放感のあるやきとん屋なのです。中に入ると外から見た以上に広めでゆったりしていてカウンター席とテーブル席含めて20人は座れそうです。

　ご主人は常連さんからは佳代ちゃんという名で親しまれている焼きトン屋には珍しい若い女性です。その佳代ちゃんが一串一串丁寧に焼いてくれます。オープンは4年目というから新しい店です。「梅ちゃん」ってのはやはり梅屋敷だから。オススメは味噌ダレ味のやきとんともつ煮です。

東京都大田区蒲田1-3-4　川畑ビル1階

営　夕方5時から深夜12時まで
休　水曜日
Tel　03-6424-8420

アクセス
京浜急行梅屋敷駅を出て踏切は渡らずに「ぷらもーる梅屋敷商店街」を200㍍程真っ直ぐ、大通りも越えてファミレスとクリーニング屋さんの間を入ってしばらく歩いた左側。赤い暖簾が目印。

42 Okamechaya

Shibuya **Izakaya**

This place lies on the corner of Shinsen vicinity where love hotels are everywhere. It's an area for adults. Okamechaya possesses a Showa atmosphere. After opening the sliding door, you are greeted by a beautiful mama san dressed in traditional work garment. According to her, this Izakaya has been around for 20 some years. There are counter, tables and semi-private open seats in the back. Accommodates about 25 people altogether.

The fact that mama san is from Hakata, the menu is full of home-style dishes with Kyushu and Okinawa ingredients. Her hobby is fishing so sometimes the menu includes dishes using the fish she caught.

Matsubara Corporate 1F 19-11 Maruyamachō Shibuya-ku, Tokyo-to

Open
6:00pm-2:00am
Closed
Sunday and Holidays
Tel. 03-3476-0795

Direction
Walk up the Dogenzaka from JR Shibuya Station. Turn right at the corner of the police box and destination located to your left after entering Sangyo Street. 5-6 minutes walk

おかめ茶屋

`渋谷`　　`居酒屋`

　ラブホ街だけにあってしっとりとした大人の雰囲気が漂う神泉の一角にあるのが同店。昭和ムード漂う和風居酒屋です。引き戸を開けて中に入ると作務衣姿の美人ママが迎えてくれます。聞けばもうすぐ20数年になる老舗です。店内はカウンターの席にテーブル２卓、そして奥には隠れ座敷まであって、25人は入れそうです。

　メニューを見ると、博多出身のママさんだけに九州や沖縄食材を使った家庭料理が並んでいます。また釣りが趣味で何と実際にママさんが磯釣りで釣った魚もメニューに並ぶこともあります。

東京都渋谷区円山町19-11
松原コーポ１階

営 夕方６時から翌２時
休 日曜日・祝日
TEL 03-3476-0795

アクセス
ＪＲ渋谷駅から道玄坂を上がり、右側にある交番の角を右に三業通りを入った左側。徒歩５〜６分。

43 Umeezu

Shinbashi **Izakaya**

A bit surprised to find an Izakaya on the first floor of such building. Yet, it's a real Izakaya with a noren at the doorstep. Once inside, you will see a good size U-shaped counter. This place is run by a beautiful lady chef wearing glasses.

This lady chef has a very down to earth personality which makes everyone relax. It's almost like dining at a friend's house. Recommended dish is the motsu stew cooked in skewers which is rare. According to her, many young office workers come here alone after work for a drink and dinner before heading home.

Chef's friendly character makes it easy for everyone to talk to her. Due to its location, although the customers are primary office workers, being a little away from Shinbashi Station, it is utilized as a hideout spot for those with important post.

4 Chome 21-7 Shinbashi Minato-ku, Tokyo-to

Open
6:00pm-11:00pm
Closed
Saturday, Sunday, and Holidays
Tel. 03-5500-4100

Direction
Exit at the steam locomotive side of JR Shinbashi Station. Walk along the guardrails toward Shinagawa direction. Turn right after running into Daiichi-Keihin. The first floor of the building where there is a Hoppy banner.

美味え津゛（うめづ）

新橋　　　居酒屋

　こんなビルの１階に居酒屋さんがあるのにはビックリ。一応ちゃんと暖簾もかかっていて本格的ですよ。中に入ると、程良い広さのコの字のカウンターにメガネ美人のママがいるお店です。

　ママさんの気さくなキャラがリラックスさせてくれます。何だか知り合いの家の広めの台所でくつろいでいる気分で妙に落ち着けます。オススメのモツ煮込みはこの辺じゃ珍しく串で頂けるスタイルです。聞けばひとりで来て一杯飲みながら夕食も済ませて帰る若いＯＬさんも多いみたいです。

　ママさんの人柄もあって客同士がスグ打ち解けて馴染みになるとのこと。場所柄、サラリーマン客は多いのですが、新橋駅から少し外れにあるため、役職についてるお偉いさんも隠れ家的に利用されているみたいです。

東京都港区新橋4-21-7

営 夕方６時から１１時まで
休 土曜・日曜・祝日
TEL 03-5500-4100

アクセス
ＪＲ新橋駅からＳＬ側に出て、ガード沿いを品川方向に歩いて、第一京浜にぶつかると右へちょい行くとホッピーの幟があるビルの１階。

44 Sakedokoro Nagomi

Shinagawa　**Izakaya**

Located at a Takanawaguchi near Shinagawa Station where many high-rise resort hotels are built. There is a building nearby with several old fashioned restaurants decorated with red lanterns. Some have been in this neighborhood for a long time.

If you take the stairs down to the basement, you will find yourself in a hallway where time seems to have stopped and the air is drifting with Showa odor. Restaurants ranging from Yakiton to bars. Among them is a place called Nagomi with an 8 people counter and tables that sit 14 people. The kitchen behind is managed by a nice husband and wife couple. This place offers no menu. It is an omakase style diner which means leave it to the chef. Small dishes of food are served one after another. Japanese dishes that pair well with sake. For a 3 hour limit at a price of ¥3,500 yen, you can get all you can eat and drink.

Shinagawa building Underground 1F
3 Chome 26-33 Takanawa Minato-ku, Tokyo-to

Open
4:00pm-11:30pm
Closed
Saturday, Sunday, and Holidays
Tel. 03-3441-3939

Direction
Take the JR Keikyu Shinagawa Station Takanawa exit. The building is located behind the police box where the first floor has a Pachinko store. Destination at the first floor basement of the building.

酒処・和(なごみ)

`品川`　　`居酒屋`

　この品川駅の高輪口といえば高層ホテルが建ち並んだ地区。とても盛り場があるとは思えませんが、意外にも赤提灯が灯る渋い飲み屋が集まるテナントビルが昔から駅のスグ近くにありました。

　地下へ階段を降りればそこは居酒屋あり、焼きトン屋あり、バーなどの飲食店が並ぶフロアーでこの空間だけ時間が止まったみたいな昭和の零囲気が漂っています。

　そんな中にあるのがカウンター8席に14名は座れるテーブル席と程良い広さの同店。そのカウンターの中の厨房には、仲の良いご夫婦が切り盛りしています。この店の一番の特徴はつまみのメニューが無いこと。

いわゆるお任せのシステムです。次から次へと出てくる小鉢に入った和食を中心とした料理を肴にお酒を頂くというもの。ただし3時間3500円(税込飲み放題食べ放題・ビールは1人1本まで。日本酒・焼酎は2人で1升まで。洋酒は2人でボトル1本までOK)。沢山飲みたい人はお得かもしれません。

東京都港区高輪
3-26-33
品川ビル地下1階

営 夕方4時から11時30分まで
休 土日祝日
TEL 03-3441-3939

アクセス
JR・京急品川駅高輪口を出て、右にある交番の裏の1階がパチンコ屋の入っているビルの地下1階。

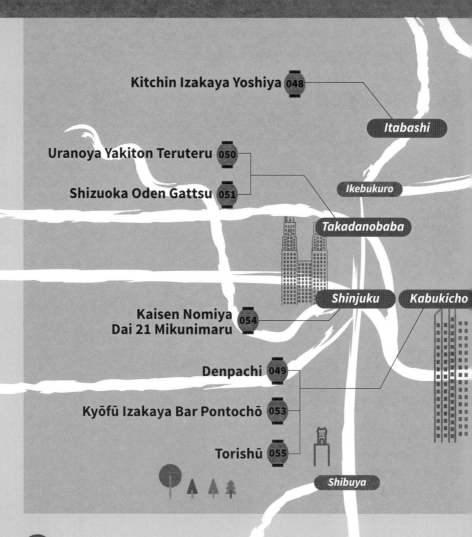

Itabashi-ku （板橋区）
Kita-ku （北区）
Toshima-ku （豊島区）
Bunkyō-ku （文京区）
Shinjuku-ku （新宿区）

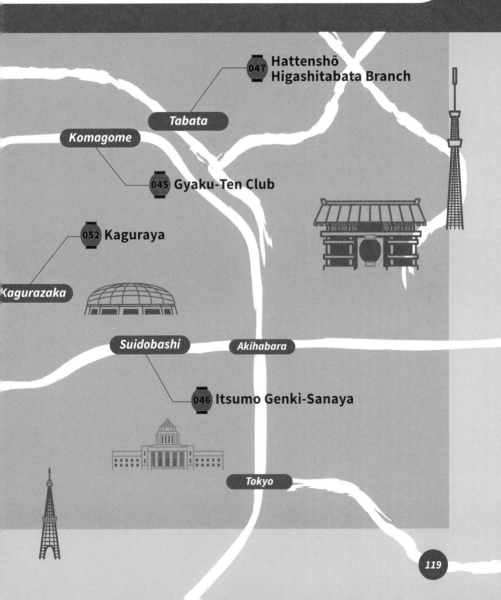

45 Gyaku-Ten Club

Komagome — **Stand and Drink Bar**

Tachinomi, or drinking while standing up, has long been a part of salaryman culture. The name Gyaku-Ten means reversal. If you stop and look inside, the place is packed with local middle-aged white collar businessmen. You might think it's hard for tourists to go here, but surprisingly, it is very cozy and welcoming.

Generally it's cash on delivery or pay as you order. The owner, Mr. Hara, has been in the food business in Komagome area for 38 years. His 5th year at this location.

"My generation has experienced the baby boomers bubble economy and also the long recession. I started this place in the spirit that despite the hardship, things are reversible."

That's the reasoning behind why he named this place Gyaku-Ten Club. While the customers are primarily an older crowd, this is an unique standing bar where one can experience old-town Tokyo and the taste of delicious grilled yakitori chicken.

---

2 Chome 7-19 Komagome Toshima-ku, Tokyo-to

Open
5:00pm-11:00pm
Closed
Once per month on Sunday
Tel. N/A

Direction
Turn left at JR Komagome Station east exit. After passing Satsuki Street shopping district, turn left at the main street. It's in front of a men's clothing store.

逆転クラブ

駒込　　**立ち飲み**

何やら気になる店名に、つい立ち止まって中を覗くと、地元のオヤジ連中がギッシリ。初めての客は奥の方まで入り辛い雰囲気ですが、これが意外に和やかなムードで居心地がいいのです。

基本はキャッシュオンデリバリー。御店主の原さんは地元駒込で飲食店を始めてすでに38年。この場所では5年目だとか。

「我々団塊の世代はバブルも長い不景気も経験してるけど、まだまだ逆転するという心意気でこの店を始めたんですよ」

だそうで、どうやらその心意気が店名の由来みたい

です。実際に客は年配客のオヤジばかりで東京の下町風情と焼き鳥が味わえるこれぞオーソドックスな立ち飲みと言える一軒です。

東京都豊島区駒込2-7-19

営　夕方5時〜11時まで
休　毎月1回だけ日曜日
個　ナシ

アクセス
ＪＲ駒込駅前東口を出て左へ。さつき通り商店街を抜けて大通りを左へ曲がってスグ。紳士服屋さんの手前。

46 Itsumo Genki-Sanaya

Suidobashi **Izakaya**

From the main street down the stairs to the basement, one will be surprised by how spacious this Izakaya is.

Immediately to the left, there is a U-shaped counter, and on the right, sit down tables are available. The capacity is about 30 people. The atmosphere of the restaurant is a mixture of Western and Japanese styles. It is a place everyone can enjoy, even for people who come here by themselves.

Suidobashi is a popular area, busy with people from everywhere. Visitors ranging from domestic and foreign travelers, local students, office workers to those who come on a business trip during the weekends.

The restaurant offers an extensive menu. Their tuna is said to be excellent. It is definitely recommended if you want to taste fresh sashimi at a reasonable price.

AU Nan'yo-do building B1F
1 Chome 14-4
Bunkyo-ku, Hongo, Tokyo-to

Open
4:00pm-2:00am
Closed
2nd Monday of the month
Tel. 03-3868-3738

Direction
Exit at JR Suidobashi Station east exit. Looking at Tokyo Dome to the left, walk straight at Hakusan Street for 3 minutes. It will be on the right side. Immediate left at Toei Mita Line Suidobashi Station A6 exit.

いつも元気・さなや

水道橋　　**居酒屋**

通りから地下への階段をストトンと降りると、意外や意外、そこは広々とした居酒屋さんで驚かされます。

入ればスグ左側にU字のカウンター席があって、右にはゆったり座れるテーブル席。30人ぐらいのキャパです。雰囲気的には洋風のような、和風のような、独り飲みでも充分落ち着いて飲めそうです。

ここ水道橋周辺は、団体客や外国人観光客、それに学生やサラリーマンが多く、週末には地方からの出張組と色んなお客さんが訪れるとのこと。

それにしてもさすがここのメニューは豊富。中でも同店の自慢はマグロ。リーズナブルにお刺身で味わいたいならオススメです。

東京都文京区本郷1-14-4
ＡＵ南陽堂ビルＢ１Ｆ

営 夕方４時から深夜２時
休 毎月第２月曜日
TEL 03-3868-3738

[アクセス]
ＪＲ水道橋駅は東口に出て、東京ドームを左に見て白山通りを真っ直ぐ行った右側。徒歩３分。都営三田線水道橋駅Ａ６出口出てすぐ左。

47 Hattenshō Higashitabata Branch

Tabata **Izakaya**

It has long been difficult to establish business around Tabata Station where bullet train garage takes up majority of space around the station. A few eateries are found right across the bridge from the train garage. Among them is a casual Japanese diner, Hattensho, celebrating its 18th years in business. Spacious and can easily accommodate a group of up to 60 people.

Every day this place is filled with big groups of middle-aged office workers after work. The entire menu handwritten on the blackboard is reasonably cheap.

It is said that since opening this place has been proudly served food in big portions. The recommended dish is their delicious original green onion yakisoba noodle. Topped with enormous amount of green onions. Served in large plate good for two people. Besides yakisoba, a wide range of classic menu such as sashimi, skewers, deep fried food are also available.

Imai building 1F
1 Chome 12-2 Kita-ku, Higashitabata, Tokyo-to

Open
11:00am-2:00pm & 4:30pm-12:00am
Closed
Open throughout the year
Tel. 03-3810-3445

Direction
Exit from JR Tabata Station north exit and turn right. After crossing Tabata Fureai bridge, go down the stairs where there is a coffee shop to the right side. It's in front of the police box.

八天将　東田端店

| 田端 | 居酒屋 |

　田端駅周辺は新幹線車庫があって駅前に盛り場を形成し難い所ですが、ちょうどその車庫をまたぐようにしてある公園橋を渡り切った所に数軒の居酒屋さんがあります。中でもこちらは18年目を迎える昭和の大衆酒場です。広い店内でざっと60人は余裕で入れそうなのでグループ客は安心です。

　同店は連日仕事帰りの中高年サラリーマングループ客で賑わっています。壁に掛かっている黒板に手書きされているオススメメニューどれも安い！

　この店はすでに18年も営業しているそうで、昔からボリュームタップリが自慢だとか。オススメは「元祖ネギ焼そば」。いやはやこれが何と刻まれた万能ネギで麺が見え無いぐらいに盛られています。量にして2人前はある大盛りですよ。しかも旨い！他にも串物から刺身、揚げ物と居酒屋定番メニューが揃っています。

東京都北区田端1-12-2　今井ビル1階

営　昼11時から午後2時。夕方4時30分から夜12時まで
休　年中無休
TEL　03-3810-3445

アクセス
ＪＲ田端駅北口を出て右へ。田端ふれあい橋を渡り切った右側のコーヒーショップの脇の階段を降りた交番の前。

48 Kitchin Izakaya Yoshiya

Itabashi | **Izakaya**

Kitchin Izakaya Yoshiya is a casual and popular Izakaya where locals from Itabashi area stop by. Relatively close to the station, look for a big blue noren curtain hanging down at the doorstep. Once open the sliding door, there are counters on both sides. The right one is adjacent to the kitchen which sits roughly 7 or 8. Second floor is an open space which can accommodate groups up to 12 or 13 people. The recommended dish is the beef stew cooked in celery tomato sauce using beef from a long established butcher shop in Nihonbashi and maguro tataki, (minced tuna) which uses fresh tuna from Tsukiji. The rare fatsia sprouts shochu is also very tasty so give it a try.

6 Chome 86-2 Takinogawa Kita-ku, Tokyo-to

Open
5:00pm-1:00am
Closed
Twice a month
Tel. 080-1252-1001

Direction
Exit at JR Itabashi Station east exit and turn left at the left corner of the rotary where McDonalds is located. Go straight for about 5 minutes.

キッチン居酒屋　よし屋

板橋　　**居酒屋**

　ここは地元板橋の人が気軽にフラッと立ち寄る居酒屋として人気のお店です。駅からほど近いところにあって大きな暖簾が目印です。サッシの引き戸を開けて中へ入れば、左右の壁に向かう形でカウンターがあって、右が厨房になっていて7〜8人は座れます。そして2階はお座敷になっていて12〜13人のグループ客も対応可能です。オススメは日本橋にある三代続く肉屋から仕入れる牛すじを使った牛すじのセロリトマト煮と築地から仕入れるマグロを使ったマグロのタタキ。さらには珍しい焼酎のたらの芽割りもクセがなくて美味しいのです。

東京都北区滝野川6-86-2

営　夕方5時から深夜1時まで
休　不定休（月2回）
Tel　080-1252-1001

アクセス
JR板橋駅東口を出てロータリーの左角のマックを左へ。そのまま真っ直ぐ歩いて5分程。

49 Denpachi

Kabukicho **Izakaya**

Just like Kabukicho where things have changed over time. Denpachi is an Izakaya which was established some 40 years ago. After going up the narrow staircase suddenly you will find yourself inside an old style Japanese Izakaya. A big contrast from the busy and loud streets just steps away. It takes a bit of getting used to for customers who have never been here.

Customers are mainly men in their 30s, 40s and 50s and some young women. Near the counter, regulars enjoy drinking and eating comfortably.

Sardine dish such as sashimi come highly recommended. Beef tongue menu is another popular hit at this place.

2F 1 Chome
15-8 Kabukicho
Shinjuku-ku, Tokyo-to

Open
5:00pm-12:00am
Closed
New Year
Tel. 03-3200-8003

Direction
From Shinjuku Station, enter Shinjuku Kabukicho where there is Don Quijote. Turn right at the alley of the third streak. Located on second floor. 8 minutes walk

でんハ

歌舞伎町 **居酒屋**

　時代と共に移りゆく歌舞伎町の中でもここのお店は40年以上前から営業している老舗居酒屋です。狭い間口の階段を2階に上がって店内に入ると、先程までのキラキラした街の喧噪がウソのように消えて、和風居酒屋の佇まいが広がっていきます。初めての客はまずこのギャップを体験することになるのです。

　客層は30代から50代のサラリーマンから若い女のコも目につきます。ご多分に漏れずカウンターには常連のお父さんが居心地良さそうに飲んでいます。

　オススメはお刺身などのいわし料理。また牛たん料理も同店の看板メニューなのです。

東京都新宿区歌舞伎町1-15-8・2階

営　夕方5時から12時まで。
休　年中無休（年末年始はお休み）
TEL　03-3200-8003

[アクセス]
新宿駅から新宿歌舞伎町はドンキホーテのあるところから入って行って3筋目の路地を右へ入っていったすぐ右側の2階。徒歩8分。

Uranoya Yakiton Teruteru

50

Takadanobaba | *Yakiton*

A little away from Takadanobaba Station, a red lantern with "Nikomi" written is the landmark. All staffs are dressed in the same black T-shirt.

As a yakiton eatery, this place caters many women customers. When you look at the menus, items are priced around 100 yen. From steak, french fries to seasonal vegetables and gratin, this place has just about everything to please both Japanese and foreigners.

Its skewers are cooked just right. There is no distinct smell to it so it's delicious. This place gets crowded at night, so it's best to go early.

3 Chome 22-4 Takadanobaba Shinjuku-ku, Tokyo-to

Open
5:00pm-12:00am
Closed
Monday
Tel. 03-6908-8351

Direction
Get off at Takadanobaba Station using either JR or subway. At Waseda Street, go towards Otakibashi direction. Immediately to the right after passing Ozeki supermarket. 8 minutes walk

浦野屋　やきとん てるてる

高田馬場　　**焼きトン**

　高田馬場駅からちょいと離れた所にあって"煮込み"の赤い提灯が目印です。女性店員さんがお揃いの黒のTシャツ姿で接客してくれます。

　焼きトン屋さんにしては女性客が多い。メニューを見ると、やきとん1本100円を始めとしてお安いメニューが並びます。揚げ物系からステーキに季節野菜のバーニャカウダにグラタンなんてのもあります。これは日本人も外国人にも喜ばれる"やきとんバル"といってもいいほど。やきとんは焼きすぎず絶妙な焼き具合。臭みも無くてホクホクしていて旨いのです。夜になるとすぐに満員になる人気店なので、早い時間がオススメです。

東京都新宿区高田馬場3-22-4

- 営 夕方5時から12時まで
- 休 月曜日
- TEL 03-6908-8351

【アクセス】
ＪＲ及び地下鉄高田馬場駅を出て、早稲田通りを小滝橋方面へ。スーパーオオゼキを過ぎてスグ右側。徒歩8分。

51 Shizuoka Oden Gattsu

Takadanobaba *Izakaya*

This place is specialized in Shizuoka food. Once inside, you will see a huge painting of Mt. Fuji, which represents Shizuoka, in sunset color. Both table seats and counters are available.

You can call this Izakaya a beach house of Shizuoka. Very relaxing. The chef is from Shizuoka. He opened this place two years ago. He loves his town, and is passionate about the food from there. The menu here includes dried fish and small sardines direct from Numazu. Many kind of sake including the ones brewed by Isojiman Sake Company from Shizuoka. Oden fishcakes on a stick are recommended at this place.

Abe building 1F
2 Chome 19-8
Takadanobaba
Shinjuku-ku, Tokyo-to

Open
5:00pm-1:00am Mon-Thurs.
Friday, Saturday, and Holidays opens till 5:00am, Sunday 4:00pm-11:00pm
Closed
Open throughout the year
Tel. 03-6316-8490

Direction
Exit at JR Takadanobaba Station Waseda exit. Cross the signal and enter the alley with Izakaya lined along the Seibu Line.

静岡おでん・ガッツ

高田馬場　**居酒屋**

　ここは静岡に特化した居酒屋です。中に入ると、なるほど壁にドーンと静岡のシンボルとも言える富士山、それも夕焼けに映える赤富士が描かれています。店内の席はビールケースで右に独り飲み用のカウンター席もあります。

　静岡の海の家と言ってもいいぐらいにリラックス出来ます。見ればカウンターの中の厨房にいるのがメガネの店長さん。この店を開いて２年目なんですって。

　当然のこと静岡出身で、まさに郷土愛が結実したお店なのです。メニューは見ると、沼津直送の干し魚や生しらすもあるし、日本酒も静岡の名酒（磯自慢）もあります。

　中でも串刺しになっている静岡おでんがオススメです。

東京都新宿区高田馬場2-19-8　阿部ビル１階

営　夕方５時から深夜１時。金土祝前は朝５時まで。日曜日は夕方４時から11時まで
休　年中無休
TEL　03-6316-8490

アクセス
ＪＲ高田馬場駅は早稲田口に出て、信号を渡り、西武線の線路沿いの居酒屋が並ぶ路地に入って中程。

52 Kaguraya

Kagurazaka **Izakaya**

Located at the pricy Kagurazaka area where long-established high-end restaurants and luxurious French restaurants are abundant. Many good and inexpensive Izakaya have opened here recently. Among them, Kaguraya is probably the most reasonable Izakaya you can find.

Red lantern as the landmark. It has a limited space on the first floor with just 4 tables and a slightly roomier second floor. Their menu is amazing. Rich in varieties. Fish dishes mainly, but also sushi, tempura, fried items, skewers, and even westerns.

Depending on what the ingredients they bought that day, their menu might change. You can taste delicious and fresh fish at a relatively low cost. It's so good we recommend you go hungry.

---

1 Chome 11 Kagurazaka Shinjuku-ku, Tokyo-to

Open
11:30am-2:00pm
5:00pm-last order
Closed Sunday
Tel. 03-6265-3966

Direction
Turn right at JR Iidabashi Station west exit. Climb up the hill of Kagurazaka and turn left at the first alley.

かぐら家

| 神楽坂 | 居酒屋 |

ここ神楽坂といえば老舗の料亭や高級フレンチ、イタ飯などが並び、ちょいとお高くつくエリアですが、最近は安くて  旨い居酒屋さんもけっこうオープンしています。中でも同店は恐らく神楽坂一リーズナブルな居酒屋。

目印は赤提灯です。テーブル４つの小ぢんまりとした１階と広めの２階があります。

さて、ここのメニューの種類がスゴイ。魚料理をメインに、寿司や天ぷら、フライも、更に洋食に串焼きと、バリエーション豊富です。

その日の仕入れによって魚のネタは変わりますが、新鮮な肴を比較的安くいっぱいいただくことができます。お腹を空かせてから行くのをオススメします。

東京都新宿区神楽坂1-11 ふぁーぶる1

営 昼11時30分から２時と夕方５時からラスト
休 日曜日
TEL 03-6265-3966

アクセス
ＪＲ飯田橋駅西口改札を出て右へ。神楽坂下から坂を上がって、最初の路地を左に曲がってスグ。

Kyōfū Izakaya Bar Pontochō

Kabukicho | **Izakaya**

Located inside a brick building on the first floor along with other restaurants, Pontocho will catch you by surprise. All seating is on the floor with low tables. A dining hall decorated in the traditional style Kyoto matsuri festival image. Moreover, you have to take off shoes before stepping up to the seating area. It makes you forget you are in Kabukicho.

The recommended dish is the "Pontoyaki Kujō negi-mori." Fluffy takoyaki style or more like an okominiyaki, Japanese pancake. Topped with sweet and sour Tsubame sauce which is famous in Kansai. Also try the "Oboro tofu no mentaiko yuba ankake". A creamy and a bit spicy tofu with mentaiko caviar. By the way, their tofu is from a famous brand called "Kamo Tofu Kinki" made in Kyoto.

Lion Plaza Shinjuku 1F 2 Chome 9-18 Kabukicho Shinjuku-ku, Tokyo-to

Open
Sunday and Monday 6:00pm-3:00am
Tuesday, Wednesday, and Thursday 6:00pm-6:00am
Friday and Saturday 6:00pm-7:00am

Closed
Open throughout the year

Tel. 03-3208-7271

Direction
Exit from JR Shinjuku Station to Yasukuni Street. Then go to Shinjuku Ward Office Street towards Shin-Okubo direction. Turn right at the signal where there is Fūrinkaikan. Look for a brick wall building on the left side after walking for a little bit. First floor of the building. 10 minutes walk

京風居酒屋バー・先斗町

`歌舞伎町`　　　`居酒屋`

　飲食店が数件並ぶレンガ壁のビルの１階の一番奥にあるのがこの店。中に入ってちょいと驚かされます。何とカウンターも含めて全面お座敷で、ちゃぶ台が置かれたりして純和風。なんでも京都の祭りの後の宴会場のイメージとか。それにしても玄関で靴を脱いで座敷に上がると、くつろげます。ここが歌舞伎町だってことを忘れそうです。

　さぁて、まずはオススメは「ぽんと焼九条ねぎ盛り」。ふわふわトロトロのたこ焼き風の？ いやいやお好み焼きといえばいいのか、上にかかったソースは甘さと酸味が控えめでも旨みのある、関西では有名な「つばめソース」。また「おぼろ豆腐の明太子ゆばあんかけ」。とろりとした舌触りにピリッとくる明太子がアクセントになっています。ちなみに豆腐は京都の「賀茂とうふ近喜」謹製を取り寄せています。

東京都新宿区歌舞伎町2-9-18　ライオンズプラザ新宿１階

営 夕方６時から深夜３時（日・月）朝６時まで（火・水・木）朝７時まで（金・土）
休 年中無休
TEL 03-3208-7271

[アクセス]
ＪＲ新宿駅から靖国通りへ出て新宿区役所通りへ新大久保方面に、風林会館のある信号を右へ。しばらく行った左側にあるレンガ壁のビルの１階徒歩10分程。

Kaisen Nomiya Dai 21 Mikunimaru

54

Shinjuku **Izakaya**

Speaking of entertainment center in Shinjuku 3 chome vicinity, it has been clustered in Suehiro Street neighborhood area. Located on the third floor inside an old-fashioned building, this place takes some courage for someone to go up at first.

Despite the narrow and old-fashioned image outside, once entered, you will be surprised how big this place actually is.

If you look at the back of the wall, you will see a huge fishing boat banner flag with the name of the shop raised up. In fact, the master here used to be a salmon fisherman. And before he became a fisherman, he was a member of the elite Ranger troops of Japanese Self-Defense Forces. Quite some careers there. By the way, his hobby is grass rugby.

Regular patrons say "This place is good because it has good food and good master". It is a place where groups can meet and drink without holding back.

Fujiwara second building 3F
3 Chome 12-3
Shinjuku, Shinjuku-ku, Tokyo-to

Open
5:00pm-late at night

Closed
Obon and New Year only

Tel. 03-3350-6078

Direction
Exit from JR Shinjuku Station to Yasukuni street. Go past the Shinjuku 5-chome intersection. Located immediately to the left after entering Suehiro Street.

廻船呑屋・第21みくに丸

新宿 **居酒屋**

　新宿は3丁目あたりの盛り場といえば、末広通り界隈に密集していますが、そんな中異彩を放つ古風なビルにインパクトのある看板が目印です。店へはそのビルの階段を上った3階にあります。入口がこれまた古風なスナック風のガラスのドアで、初めての人はちょいと勇気がいる感じです。

　でも中に入ると、アララ突然目の前が開けて、うって変わって大箱の居酒屋の店内が広がってビックリします。

　見れば奥の壁には、店名が染め抜かれた漁船が揚げる大漁旗が目に飛び込んできます。実はここのマスターはシャケ漁の元漁師さんでした。しかもそれ以前は精鋭無比の自衛隊のレンジャー部隊にいた変わった経歴の方です。ちなみに趣味は草ラグビーです。

　常連客曰く「この店はマスターと料理がいいから」とのことです。気兼ねなく飲めるグループ客には打って付けの居酒屋なのです。

東京都新宿区新宿3-12-3
藤原第2ビル3階

営 夕方5時から深夜まで
休 お盆と正月だけ
TEL 03-3350-6078

アクセス
JR新宿駅から靖国通りに出て、新宿5丁目交差点を過ぎて、最初の通り角を右の、末広通りを入ってスグ左側。

55 Torishū

Kabukicho **Yakitori**

A bit hidden from the Kabukicho, there is a restaurant called Torishū. Started in Meiji era as a wholesale chicken egg merchant, today, it is a yakitori restaurant. Inside, there is a 12 seat L shaped counter and a couple of tables. Accommodates 30 people. The huge beams and pillars present the feel of old Japanese house. It makes you forget that you are at Kabukicho, the red-light district.

According to the owner, their family has been a chicken wholesaler since Meiji. He is the 3rd generation. Everyday, this place is busy with locals and customers who want to enjoy good Yakitori.

Their chicken is juicy and tender with a great texture. It uses chicken raised in Chiba area called Kinso Tori. It's a masterpiece when you add spice or cheese to it.

Reokotobuki building 1F 2 Chome 41-4 Kabukicho, Shinjuku-ku, Tokyo-to

Open
5:30pm-12:00am (last order 11:00pm)
Closed
Sunday and Holidays
Tel. 03-3207-4411

Direction
Exit at Seibu Shinjuku Station north exit. Walk the Shokuan Street toward the direction of Yamate Street and turn right at the corner of Softbank. Located immediately after entering Second Street. 5-6 minutes walk

鳥修

歌舞伎町　　**焼き鳥**

　新宿歌舞伎町でも裏手というか外れの、意外な場所にあるこの店は表の看板に"明治三十五年創業の食鳥鶏卵問屋直営"と書かれています。店内は12人掛けのL字のカウンターに、奥は小上がりとテーブル席。ざっと30人は入れそうです。重厚な梁や柱が古民家のような落ち着きを演出していて、ここが歌舞伎町であることを忘れてしまいます。

　聞けば先の看板にあるように明治から続く鶏肉問屋から焼鳥屋を始めていまのご主人で三代目にあたるとのことです。連日地元の常連さんや鶏好きなお馴染みさんで賑わっています。

　鳥肉は、筋肉質で旨みがある味わい深い食感の千葉の錦爽鳥（きんそうどり）という肉。それに香辛料やチーズを乗せて焼く香味焼は絶品です。

東京都新宿区歌舞伎町2-41-4　レオ寿1階

営 夕方5時30分～12時（ラストオーダー11時）
休 日曜日・祝日
Tel 03-3207-4411

アクセス
西武新宿駅北口を出て、職安通りを山手通り方面に歩いてソフトバンクの角を右へ。二番通りに入ってスグ。歩いて5～6分程。

Appendix 1 Shinjuku Golden Gai

Shinjuku Golden Gai is a small area of Shinjuku, Tokyo, Japan, famous both as an area of architectural interest and for its nightlife. It is composed of a network of six narrow alleys, connected by even narrower passageways which are just about wide enough for a single person to pass through. Over 200 tiny shanty-style bars, clubs and eateries are squeezed into this area.

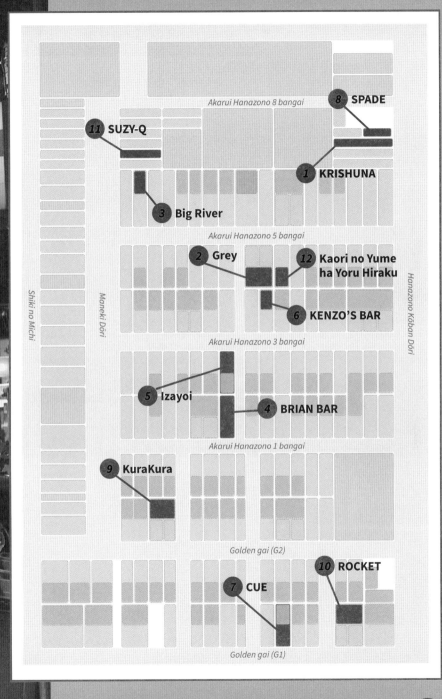

Shinjuku Golden gai

1 KRISHUNA
クリシュナ

Open 7pm ~ last order * cover charge 500 yen

Budget 2,000 ~ 2,500 yen

Middle Eastern Style theme (Balkans & Egypt) makes you forget you are in Japan. Relatively spacious interior perfect for groups.

営 19時~ラスト　※チャージ500円

予算 2000円~ 2500円

中東風（バルカン＆エジプト）なイメージはここが日本であることを忘れてしまう。比較的広い店内はグループ客にピッタリ。

2 Grey

Open 7pm ~ 2am * cover charge 1,400 yen

Budget 2,000 ~ 3,000 yen

Capacity is around 13. Quiet and consistent gray interior like its name.
Relax atmosphere makes you feel like being in a luxurious living room.

営 19時~深夜2時　※チャージ1400円

予算 2000円~ 3000円

キャパが13人ほどの静かな店内は店名通りグレーに統一されている。まるでマダムのリビングルームにいるみたいな落ち着きが支配する。

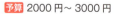

3 Big River
ビッグリバー

Open 6pm ~ last order * cover charge 1,000 yen

Budget 2,000 yen ~

The club host was previously a magazine editor. She created this space so that people working in the publishing industry can get together and have discussions without boundaries. The recommended dish is the special curry rice.

営 18時~ラスト　※チャージ1000円

予算 2000円~

元雑誌の編集長だったママが経営する同店は出版関係者が集う屈託の無い空間が支配する。オススメは同店特製のカレーライス。

4 BRIAN BAR

Open 8pm ~ 5am * cover charge 1,000 yen (tourists are free)

Budget 2,000 yen ~

Enjoy the stylish interior and have a good time talking with the friendly bartenders. This place sells cigars and smoking is allowed.

営 20時~早朝5時　※チャージ1000円（観光客はフリー）

予算 2000円~

スタイリッシュ空間にフレンドリーな店員との会話を楽しみながら時間を過ごる店。葉巻も販売していて店内でも吸える。

Shinjuku Golden gai

5 Izayoi
十六夜（いざよい）

Open 8pm ~ last order * cover charge 800 yen

Budget 2,000 yen ~

Time seems to flow slowly here. Relaxing atmosphere. A typical bar with a club host and counter seating.

営 20時〜ラスト　※チャージ800円

予算 2000円〜

ここだけは時間がゆっくりと流れているようである。リラックスした空間にはママとカウンターがあるスタンダードな一軒。

6 KENZO'S BAR

Open 8pm ~ 5am * cover charge 500 yen

Budget 700 yen ~

Master loves the leopard design. From the interior of the bar to the clothes he wears are all in leopard prints. A unique club in the Golden Street.

営 20時〜早朝5時　※チャージ500円

予算 700円〜

豹柄好きなマスターがいる同店は店内の内装からマスターの服に至るまでこれ全て豹柄。ゴールデン街の中でも異色な店。

7 CUE
灸 CUE

Open
8pm ~ 5am * cover charge 800 yen

Budget 600 yen ~

Soul blues music is playing here. Equipped with great sound system, this is a perfect spot to spend the night listening to your favorite music.

営 20時〜早朝5時　※チャージ800円

予算 600円〜

ソウルブルースのＢＧＭが店内に流れる同店。自慢はゴールデン街一音のいい音響システム。音楽に乗って夜通し過ごすのにピッタリ。

8 SPADE

Open
8pm ~ last order * cover charge 700 yen

Budget 2,000 yen ~

A bar that plays hard rock music. You can forget the hustle and bustle outside and enter another space when sitting in the passionate red walls here.

営 夜20時〜ラスト　※チャージ700円

予算 2000円〜

ハードロックのＢＧＭが店内に流れる同店。情熱的な赤い壁の内装はそれまでの外の喧噪を忘れさせ異空間へと連れていってくれる。

Shinjuku Golden gai

9 KuraKura
クラクラ

Open
7pm ~ 2am * cover charge 1,200 yen

Budget
2,000 yen ~

Both bar and Izakaya in a mountain hut like open atmosphere. Perfect for talking and debating while drinking with fellow friends.

営 19時〜翌2時　※チャージ1200円

予算 2000円〜

バーと居酒屋が一緒になったような山小屋風の開放的な空間。ワイワイガヤガヤと語らいながら仲間と飲むにはピッタリ。

10 ROCKET

Open
9pm ~ the last order *cover charge 1000 yen

Budget
2,000 yen ~

Woody atmosphere inside. Shelves are full of records and CDs. This bar plays different kind of music every day. Relax and enjoy the music of the day and good food.

営 21時〜ラスト　※チャージ1000円。

予算 2000円〜

ウッディーな空間の店内。壁にある棚にはＣＤやレコードがギッシリと納められている。日替わりで違う音楽を肴にゆったりと過ごす店だ。

11 SUZY-Q

Open
9pm ~ 5am * cover charge 1,000 yen

Budget 2,000 yen ~

Enjoy sophisticated conversations while having a glass of drink poured by the beautiful madam dressed in elegant cloth behind the counter. A good representation of the typical Golden Street bar since the old days.

営 21時〜早朝5時　※チャージ1000円

予算 2000円〜

ドレッシーな美人マダム達とカウンター越しにグラスを傾けながら洒落た大人の会話を楽しめる大人が集う昔からのゴールデン街らしい店。

12 Kaori no Yume ha Yoru Hiraku
かおりの夢ハ夜ヒラク

Open
7pm ~ 5am * cover charge 500 yen

Budget 2,000 yen ~

Customers come here to listen to the songs from showa era and to meet the cheerful club host. This bar is filled with patrons who enjoy talking and laughing while eating and drinking. A place to enjoy with everyone.

営 19時〜早朝5時　※チャージ500円

予算 2000円〜

ワイワイがやがやとカウンターにギッシリと詰めかける客は昭和歌謡と元気なママとの会話と笑いを肴に飲みにくる。みんなと楽しむためのお店。

Appendix 2 Izakaya Menu

肉料理 Meat

焼き鳥 Yakitori

Yakitori is barbecued skewered chicken and has endless variations. Almost all parts of the chicken, including the skin and internal organs, are used for yakitori.

すき焼き Sukiyaki

Sukiyaki is a hot-pot dish, and the main ingredients are sliced beef, tofu, and scallions. It is cooked in a shallow iron pot with soy sauce, sugar, mirin, or sweet cooking sake, and sake. A small bowl of raw egg is served with sukiyaki for dipping.

しゃぶしゃぶ Shabu-shabu

Shabu-shabu is a hot-pot dish, and the main ingredient is beef sliced paper-thin. Tofu and vegetables commonly accompany the meat. To enjoy shabu-shabu, people use ultra thin-beef slices cooked in a pot with boiling broth, and dipped in sauce.

とんかつ Tonkatsu

Tonkatsu is deep-fried pork cutlets.

餃子 Gyoza

Chinese ravioli-dumplings (potstickers), usually filled with pork and vegetables (spring onion, leek, cabbage, garlic, and ginger) and pan-fried. Other popular methods include boiled sui-gyoza (水餃子) and deep fried age-gyoza (揚げ餃子).

肉じゃが Nikujaga

Nikujaga is beef and potato stew, flavored with sweet soy.

唐揚げ Karaage

Karaage is bite-sized pieces of chicken, fish, octopus, or other meat, floured and deep fried.

魚料理 Fish

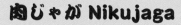

刺身 Sashimi

Sashimi is raw, thinly sliced foods served with a dipping sauce and simple garnishes; usually fish or shellfish served with soy sauce and wasabi.

南蛮漬け Nanbanzuke

Nanbanzuke is marinated fried fish.

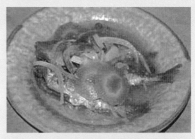

てんぷら Tempura

Tempura is deep-fried vegetables or seafood in a light, distinctive batter.

照り焼き Teriyaki

Teriyaki is grilled, broiled, or pan-fried meat, fish, chicken or vegetables glazed with a sweetened soy sauce.

蒲焼 Kabayaki

Kabayaki is a preparation of fish, especially unagi eel, [1] where the fish is split down the back [2] (or belly), gutted and boned, butterflied, cut into square fillets, skewered, dipped in a sweet soy sauce-base sauce before being broiled on a grill.

焼き魚 Yakizakana

Yakizakana is flame-grilled fish, often served with grated daikon.

Izakaya Menu

煮魚 Nizakana

Nizakana is fish poached in sweet soy.

麺類 Noodles

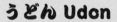

蕎麦 Soba

Soba is thin brown buckwheat noodles.

うどん Udon

Udon is thick white wheat noodles served with various toppings, usually in a hot soy-dashi broth, or sometimes in a Japanese curry soup.

ラーメン Ramen

Ramen is thin light yellow noodles served in hot chicken or pork broth with various toppings.

素麺 Somen

Somen is thin white wheat noodles served chilled with a dipping sauce. Hot Somen is called Nyumen.

焼きそば Yaki soba

Yaki soba is fried Chinese noodles.

丼 Rice Bowls

カツ丼 Katsudon

Katsudon is donburi topped with deep-fried breaded cutlet of pork.

牛丼 Gyudon

Gyudon is donburi topped with seasoned beef.

Izakaya Menu

親子丼 Oyakodon

Oyakodon is donburi topped with chicken and egg.

天丼 Tendon

Tendon is donburi topped with tempura.

漬物
Pickled or salted foods

いくら Ikura

Ikura is salt cured and pickled soy sauce salmon caviar.

たらこ Tarako

Tarako is salt-cured cod roe or pollock roe.

塩辛 Shiokara

Shiokara is salty fermented viscera.

漬物 Tsukemono

Tsukemono is pickled vegetables, hundreds of varieties and served with most rice-based meals.

その他の惣菜
Miscellaneous side dish

おでん Oden

Oden is a Japanese winter dish consisting of several ingredients such as boiled eggs, daikon, konjac, and processed fishcakes stewed in a light, soy-flavored dashi broth.

枝豆 Edamame

Edamame is boiled and salted pods of soybeans, eaten as a snack, often to accompany beer.

冷奴　Hiyayakko

Hiyayakko is chilled tofu with garnish.

納豆　Natto

Natto is fermented soybeans, stringy like melted cheese, infamous for its strong smell and slippery texture.

A Guide to Japanese Pubs and Izakaya
東京居酒屋ガイド

2015年8月8日　第1刷発行

著　者　　島本慶 & SKIP

発行者　　浦　晋　亮

発行所　　IBCパブリッシング株式会社
　　　　　〒162-0804 東京都新宿区中里町29番3号 菱秀神楽坂ビル9F
　　　　　Tel. 03-3513-4511 Fax. 03-3513-4512
　　　　　www.ibcpub.co.jp

印刷所　　株式会社シナノパブリッシングプレス

© IBC パブリッシング 2015
Printed in Japan

落丁本・乱丁本は、小社宛にお送りください。送料小社負担にてお取り替えいたします。
本書の無断複写（コピー）は著作権法上での例外を除き禁じられています。

ISBN978-4-7946-0359-3